HOUSE OF COMMONS                SES

# TRADE AND INDUSTRY COMMITTEE

Tenth Report

# ELECTRONIC COMMERCE

Report, together with the
Proceedings of the Committee
and Appendices

---

*Ordered by* The House of Commons *to be printed*
*15 July 1999*

---

LONDON: THE STATIONERY OFFICE
£11·50

HC 648

The Trade and Industry Committee is appointed under Standing Order No 152 to examine the expenditure, administration and policy of the Department of Trade and Industry and associated public bodies.

The Committee consists of 11 Members. It has a quorum of three. Unless the House otherwise orders, all members nominated to the Committee continue to be members of it for the remainder of the Parliament.

The Committee has power:

(a)    to send for persons, papers and records, to sit notwithstanding any adjournment of the House, to adjourn from place to place, and to report from time to time;

(b)    to appoint specialist advisers either to supply information which is not readily available or to elucidate matters of complexity within the Committee's order of reference;

(c)    to communicate to any other committee appointed under the same Standing Order (and to the Committee of Public Accounts, Deregulation Committee, Environmental Audit Committee and European Scrutiny Committee) its evidence and any other documents relating to matters of common interest; and

(d)    to meet concurrently with any other such committee or the European Scrutiny Committee or any sub-committee thereof for the purposes of deliberating, taking evidence, or (in the case of any other such committee) considering draft reports.

---

The membership of the Committee since its nomination on 9 July 1997 has been as follows:

Mr Martin O'Neill (Chairman)

Mr Tony Baldry
Mr John Bercow (*added 15.6.98 and discharged 5.7.99*)
Mr Roger Berry
Mr John Butterfill
Mr Christopher Chope (*added 5.7.99*)
Mr Jim Cunningham
Mr Lindsay Hoyle (*added 19.2.98*)
Mr Alan Johnson (*discharged 19.2.98*)

Mr Bob Laxton
Gillian Merron (*discharged 9.11.98*)
Mr Alasdair Morgan
Linda Perham (*added 22.6.98*)
Mr David Prior (*discharged 15.6.98*)
Mrs Helen Southworth (*added 9.11.98*)
Joan Walley (*discharged 22.6.98* )

Mr Martin O'Neill was elected Chairman on 16 July 1997.

---

# TABLE OF CONTENTS

*Page*

*From the contents of the Seventh Report of the Committee, HC 187*

Note: References to "*Q*" are to the question numbers in oral evidence, published with our previous Report on electronic commerce (98/99, HC 187). "*Ev, p*" refers to pages in the memoranda published with, or as appendices to, the oral evidence. References to "Ev, p" are to the memoranda published as appendices to this Report.

# LIST OF APPENDICES
# TO THE REPORT

*Page*

*Submitted by*

# TENTH REPORT

**The Trade and Industry Committee has agreed to the following Report:—**

## ELECTRONIC COMMERCE

### I INTRODUCTION

1. Electronic commerce, and its economic, social and other implications for the UK, have been an increasing concern of Government in recent years. The Government set out its broad ideas on "how to enable people to take advantage of the new information age" in April 1998. Its coordinated strategy is intended to focus on "transforming education, widening access, promoting competition and competitiveness, fostering quality and modernising government".[1] Several strands of this strategy are being taken forward by the Department of Trade and Industry (DTI). Measures relating to electronic commerce feature prominently in the December 1998 Competitiveness White Paper. DTI and its executive agencies are working to ensure that all of its services are capable of electronic delivery by 2008.[2] DTI also announced in April 1998 its intention to legislate to promote the legal recognition of electronic signatures and to create a voluntary licensing regime for firms offering cryptographic services including electronic signatures and encryption, following consultation of interested parties.[3] This legislation was announced in the Queen's Speech in November 1998.[4]

2. We decided on 3 December 1998 to launch a wide-ranging inquiry into electronic commerce, focusing on those aspects of policy within DTI's remit, but also considering broader issues of relevance to UK consumers and firms. We heard evidence from e centre[UK], the Confederation of British Industry (CBI) and the Federation of Small Businesses on 26 January 1999; British Telecommunications plc (BT), the Federation of the Electronics Industry, the Computing Software and Services Association and the Internet Service Providers' Association on 2 February; the National Consumer Council, Mr. Chris Reed, Head of the Information Technology Law Unit and Deputy Director of the Centre for Commercial Law Studies, Queen Mary and Westfield College, University of London, and the Association of Payment and Clearing Services (APACS) on 23 February; the National Criminal Intelligence Service and HM Customs and Excise, the Office of Telecommunications (OFTEL), the Post Office and Dr. Ross Anderson, Leader, Computer Security Group, University of Cambridge Computer Laboratory on 2 March; the Data Protection Registrar and Cyber-Rights and Cyber-Liberties (UK) on 9 March; and from DTI on 17 March. We visited British Telecommunications plc and the National Criminal Intelligence Service and also benefited from other informal briefings. We are grateful for all of the oral and written evidence we have received, including that submitted after the publication of our previous Report on electronic commerce and published with this Report,[5] and for the expert advice and assistance afforded to us by our specialist adviser for this inquiry, Mr. Peter Sommer, Research Fellow of the Computer Security Research Centre, London School of Economics.

3. We published a Report on the contents of the DTI consultation document "Building Confidence in Electronic Commerce" on 19 May 1999.[6] The Report dealt with the issues of electronic authentication and encryption, which were to be the subject of the legislation promised in the Queen's Speech. DTI said in March 1999 that the Electronic Commerce Bill would be

---

[1] *Our Information Age*, URN 98/768 — on the internet at www.number-10.gov.uk

[2] *Our Competitive Future: Building the Knowledge Driven Economy*, DTI, Dec 98, Cm 4176 (hereafter *CWP*); and for various recent DTI electronic commerce initiatives see the following press notices — 98/854, 98/920, 98/942, 98/970, 98/1035, 99/63, 99/171, 99/174, 99/312, 99/376, 99/441, 99/524, 99/539

[3] DTI Press Notice 98/320, 27 Apr 98

[4] HC Deb, 24 Nov 98, c4

[5] References to evidence printed with the previous Report are made in italics — for instance *Q55, Ev, p200 paragraph 2.5*. References to evidence printed with this volume are made in the usual way, without italics

[6] Trade and Industry Committee, Seventh Report, 1998/99, *"Building Confidence in Electronic Commerce": The Government's Proposals*, HC187

introduced to Parliament in May 1999.[7] When we published our Report we expected the Bill, and the Government's reply to our Report, to be published shortly after the Whitsun recess. We were still awaiting both the Bill and the Government's reply to us when we agreed this Report, on 15 July 1999, and we have therefore been unable to respond to either of them.

4. This Report deals with many of the issues other than authentication and encryption raised with us by witnesses, not least the need to ensure that the potential benefits of electronic commerce can be shared by all members of society. We noted that many of the issues raised with us — particularly in relation to taxation, consumer protection, privacy and intellectual property rights — were not entirely unfamiliar and that electronic commerce had introduced new dimensions to existing debates. The question of how, if at all, Government should respond to these new challenges is one we have examined in some detail. Our focus has been primarily on electronic commerce conducted over the internet, which has raised many new public policy questions, rather than on issues associated with often long–established closed networks such as the Electronic Data Interchange (EDI) system.[8] One significant issue that we did not consider during the course of our inquiry was the question of the regulation of the content of internet websites, or related on-line material. The Culture, Media and Sport Committee recently reported on this issue;[9] a statement of Government policy on this issue has also recently been published.[10]

5. We gleaned many new insights which have informed the preparation of this Report during our visit to the United States between 23–28 May. We met with representatives of the US Department of Commerce, America On-Line and others at a round table on electronic commerce at the British Embassy in Washington DC on 24 May; with the US internet service provider Earthlink on 25 May; with the mobile telephone firm Qualcomm on 26 May; with a range of electronic commerce participants and experts during a day's visit to Silicon Valley on 27 May, including the on-line auction firm eBay and Hewlett Packard; and with mobile telephone firm Airtouch Communications and Wells Fargo Bank, a major internet banking firm, in San Francisco on 28 May. We also benefited from several informal discussions with policy makers, opinion formers and business leaders. During the inquiry we also discussed electronic commerce issues with officials from both DGXIII of the European Commission and the United Nations Economic Commission for Europe.

**Opportunities and Threats**

6. We indicated in our first Report on electronic commerce that we consider three broad sets of transactions, which rely directly on computers, to comprise electronic commerce, namely:
— business to consumer transactions
— business to business transactions
— citizen to Government transactions.

Most electronic commerce is conducted between businesses. In 1998 it is estimated that $43 billion of business to business electronic commerce was transacted worldwide and it is currently predicted that this will increase to $300 billion by 2002.[11] Much of this trade is well-established, making use of closed networks such as the EDI system rather than open-networks such as the internet.[12] Electronic commerce between businesses and consumers is currently less significant — perhaps worth $7 billion worldwide in 1998 — but is growing rapidly and is expected to total as much as $80 billion in 2002.[13] Business to consumer electronic commerce has been the source of considerable comment and speculation, much of it exaggerated.[14] Citizen to Government

---

[7] *Competitiveness White Paper Implementation Plan*, DTI, Mar 99, URN99/665 (hereafter *CWP Implementation*), section D9

[8] For issues associated with closed networks see, for instance, *Qq81–2; Ev, pp1–20, p53 annex 1 paragraph A1.8, p255 paragraph 3.22, pp275–6 section 5, p287*

[9] Culture, Media and Sport Committee, Fourth Report, Session 1997/98, *The Multi-Media Revolution*, HC520

[10] *Regulating Communications: the way ahead*, DTI and DCMS, Jun 99, URN 99/898, paragraphs 3.20–3.23

[11] *Q13* and see *Ev, p259*

[12] Paragraph 7

[13] *The Emerging Digital Economy II*, US Department of Commerce, Jun 99, p5 and see *Ev, p259*

[14] For instance see *Sunday Times*, 8 Nov 98, p3:11 "Shopping on the net is posed to change face of retailing"; *Daily Telegraph*, 20 Dec 98, pB4 "Learning to live with the e-commerce monster"; *The Times*, 11 Jan 99, p44, "Internet shopping 'set to boom'"; *Guardian*, 11 Jan 99, p13, "By July, cyberspace malls will be twice as busy"; *Guardian*, 16 Jun 99, p8 "Internet 'heralds new industrial revolution'"; and also *Financial Times*, 4 Jun 99, p30 "Philips snubs price 'hype' over internet"

electronic commerce encompasses a wide range of transactions, from Government procurement to the electronic submission of tax returns, electronic voting and the communication of information between citizens and Government departments. The Government's Central Information Technology Unit has recently published a summary of the progress made by each Whitehall department in permitting its transactions with the public to be carried out electronically, which can be compared with the targets set out in the Modernising Government White Paper.[15] In the US we were made aware of a fourth form of electronic commerce, consumer to consumer transactions, including on-line auctions facilitated by firms such as eBay.[16]

7. Also in our first Report on this subject, we outlined some of the potential benefits of electronic commerce including:[17]
— increased competition, choice and convenience for consumers
— a new way of overcoming barriers to social inclusion
— low cost access to global markets and productivity gains for firms
— more efficient and convenient transactions between Government and citizens
— greater efficiency and coordination within Government
— productivity and competitiveness gains for the UK economy as a whole.

The possibility of these benefits being enjoyed within a few years from now, as a result of the rapid take-up of computer technology, particularly the internet, throughout society have excited policy makers and commentators. The Government has frequently referred to the revolutionary nature of the "knowledge driven economy", heralded by the internet, which will fundamentally alter economic inter-relationships.[18] There has been speculation that increased global competition will drive UK prices down;[19] that homeworking will increasingly replace traditional work patterns, obviating the need for workers to live within commuting distance of their employers;[20] and that Government will become more closely in touch with its electors.[21]

8. There has been less attention paid to the potential disadvantages of electronic commerce, although their existence is recognised by the Government.[22] The Computing Services and Software Association warned that "the US could become the "out of town shopping mall" that bankrupts our high street."[23] We received a useful memorandum from Age Concern on the ways in which older people might be disadvantaged as a result of the increased significance of electronic commerce.[24] The Institute of Chartered Accountants in England and Wales raised the problem of "data overload" caused by the amount of information which can be made immediately available by electronic mail and the internet.[25] We discussed with several witnesses the problems posed by electronic commerce to various sectors of the economy, including intermediaries such as travel agents and sectors reliant on intellectual property rights, such as copyright, which might be more easily infringed on-line.[26] e centre[UK] warned us that "many UK companies, especially small and medium sized enterprises, are still complacent about the threats to their businesses if they do not take up the opportunities offered by electronic commerce".[27] Some of the activities which are likely to thrive on-line may raise moral questions. In the US we were informed that internet gambling revenues were expected to total $100 billion by 2006 and that over two thirds of the revenue currently derived from the content of websites was generated

---

[15] *Progress Report: Electronic Government 25% Target,* Cabinet Office, May 99; see paragraph 93

[16] www.ebay.co.uk

[17] Paragraph 5; and see *Financial Times,* 6 Feb 99, p8 on the possible benefits to Government of electronic commerce

[18] DTI press notice 98/732, 28 Sep 98; 98/854, 4 Nov 98; 98/953, 27 Nov 98

[19] For instance see *Guardian,* section 2, p14, 10 Jun 99, "Will the internet kill Britain's car cartels"; and Trade and Industry Committee, Eighth Report, Session 1998/99, *Trade Marks, Fakes and Consumers,* HC380, Q379

[20] *Ev, p298 section 9* and for a related point see *Ev, p282*

[21] *Modernising Government,* Cabinet Office, Mar 99, Cm4310, p46; Cabinet Office, Office of Public Service, press notices 17/97, 3 Mar 97; 34/97, 18 Jun 97; 39/97, 26 Jun 97; 139/98, 8 Jun 98

[22] *Ev, p194 paragraph 2.5*

[23] *Ev, p75 section 3*; also see *Q183*

[24] *Ev, pp326–7 especially Section 3*

[25] *Ev, p279*

[26] *Qq57, 422*; *Ev, p152 section 1, p265 paragraph 7*; on threats, and opportunities, relating to the City of London see *The Future Use of Electronic Technology in Cash Transactions, Banking and Share Trading,* The Real Time Club, Jan 99; and see paragraphs 76 and 107

[27] *Ev, p4 section 8*

by pornography.

9. **It is important that, when considering how best the Government should respond to the growth of electronic commerce, potential advantages and disadvantages of the phenomenon are kept in perspective.** Most electronic transactions involve ordering physical goods which are then delivered by traditional means. While electronic ordering might be convenient for some, the costs and time delays caused by physical delivery, particularly from abroad, means that electronic commerce does not necessarily represent a revolutionary step forward from conventional mail-order. Use of the internet is, at least at present, dependent upon the use of computer equipment and software which many people might find challenging in themselves. The internet is itself a bewildering and disorganised array of interlinked pages of information, much of it obscure and trivial mostly produced by and for Americans, on which it can be fiendishly difficult to find specific items of information. We were struck by the comment of the Federation of Small Businesses that "one of the single biggest complaints that we have had from people once they get on the web is "yes, loads of information, where is the index?"[28] Finally as we will discuss later, although the Government may be able to make many of its services available electronically, that is no guarantee that the targets of these services will wish to or be able to abandon traditional forms of communication.[29]

10. Electronic commerce is but one aspect of a number of social and economic trends of the twentieth century, including the diminution of distance as an impediment to effective communication and the replacement of manufacturing industry by knowledge or skills based service industries in developed countries. Like the telephone, radio and television before it, electronic commerce is likely to become an important part of everyday life in the twenty-first century. But although it may revolutionize some aspects of life, other areas are likely to be largely unaffected. Some of the more ambitious claims made about electronic commerce, including that it might overcome social exclusion and eliminate international price differences, seem to us to be unduly ambitious. **Policy makers must be careful not to be carried away by the hyperbole and exaggeration which has, at times, come to characterise the debate on the future development of electronic commerce. Nor should their focus stray from those aspects of society which are unlikely to be touched by electronic commerce or which may be in some way damaged by it. Electronic commerce must not be regarded as a panacea for every difficult issue facing politicians today nor as the issue which most firms and individuals will believe to be most relevant to their daily lives. Nevertheless, DTI, perhaps more than any other Government department, must increasingly seek to promote the positive benefits of electronic commerce, particularly in terms of its potential impact on UK competitiveness, and at the same time seek to alleviate its drawbacks.**

## Where does the UK stand?
DEFINING ELECTRONIC COMMERCE

11. The Government has "set out the ambitious goal of developing the UK as the world's best environment for electronic trading by the end of this Parliament".[30] In order to achieve this aim it is necessary to consider where the UK stands at the moment in relation to its international competitors. It was clear to us during our inquiry that, although a number of broad estimates of the value of global electronic commerce today and in the next five years have been made, reliable, detailed statistics about electronic commerce are hard to come by. One difficulty with measuring electronic commerce has been the lack of consistency in the definition of the activity, something to which we drew attention in our previous Report.[31] **We recommend that the Government consider how electronic commerce should be defined, in order to facilitate comparison between the growth of electronic commerce in the UK and abroad.**

---

[28] *Q90*
[29] Paragraphs 95 and 97
[30] *Ev, p193 paragraph 1.1*
[31] See *paragraph 4*

ELECTRONIC COMMERCE STATISTICS

12. The DTI published an "initial snapshot" of where the UK stood in relation to a handful of major economies in December 1998 and has since published a more detailed analysis of the use made of information and communications technologies by businesses in the UK, US, Canada, Japan, France, Germany and Italy.[32] This represents welcome progress but the Minister admitted in oral evidence that more needed to be done. He argued that international benchmarking would be one of the functions of the e-envoy, when appointed.[33]

13. A whole range of statistical measures taking account of electronic commerce, in a national as well as an international context, need to be developed. We were alerted to the possibility that retail sales figures, which currently do not include on-line purchases, might give misleading signals to economic policy makers as electronic commerce becomes more popular, similar to the recent problems associated with the impact of the Average Earnings Index on monetary policy.[34] The US Secretary of Commerce recently stated that, although his Department had "begun to systematically collect data on electronic commerce, specifically on retail sales using the internet, we are still studying how to ensure that the statistical information provided by the government takes into account the stunning upheavals brought about by the internet".[35] **We recommend that the Government Statistical Service consider how best to develop new statistical measures relating to electronic commerce and to adopt its existing measures to the phenomenon.**

BENCHMARKING

14. In December 1998, along with the Competitiveness White Paper, DTI published a comparison of the UK's performance with that of other leading industrial nations on several aspects of electronic commerce.[36] This pulled together various recent published research, including the 1998 Benchmarking Study commissioned by DTI, and a subjective assessment by the business-led Information Age Partnership of where the UK stood in relation to other major industrial countries on a range of variables. The Report showed that:

— on-line trading in the UK in 1998 amounted to around 0.05% of GDP, comparable with Germany and Japan, but well behind the US[37]

— 15% of the UK's adult population had visited the World Wide Web, compared to 37% of US adults, 10% of German adults and 8% of French adults.[38] More recent research has suggested that 3 million people began to use the internet between December 1998 and June 1999 and that 21% of the UK adult population has now been on–line[39]

— UK firms were on a par with their foreign counterparts in terms of the ownership of information and communications technology equipment, but did not necessarily use it to its best advantage[40]

— the UK's strengths were its information and communications technology infrastructure, relatively low telecommunications prices and pro-competition regulatory structure; its weaknesses were high prices in some key sectors, below-par user skills and disappointing macroeconomic performance.[41]

15. The 1999 Benchmarking Study, published in April, gave fresh details about the commitment of UK firms to electronic commerce, in relation to firms in other G7 countries. Key findings included that:

---

[32] *Benchmarking the Digital Economy*, DTI, Dec 98, URN98/1037; *Moving into the Information Age 1999: International Benchmarking Study*, DTI, Apr 99, URN99/797 (hereafter *Benchmarking*) — regional and sectoral benchmarking studies were published simultaneously with this volume

[33] *Q527*; see paragraph 32 on the e-Envoy

[34] For instance see Treasury Committee, First Report, 1998–99 , *Office for National Statistics*, HC43-I; and also *BBC Online*, "Chancellor launches earnings probe", 23 Oct 98

[35] *The Emerging Digital Economy II*, US Department of Commerce, Jun 99, introduction by William M. Daley

[36] *Benchmarking the Digital Economy*, DTI, Dec 98, URN98/1037; other benchmarking studies exist of which one of the more comprehensive is *Economic and Social Impacts of Electronic Commerce: Preliminary Findings and Recent Agenda*, OECD, 1998

[37] *Benchmarking* figure 4

[38] *Benchmarking* paragraph 2.1; and see *The Emerging Digital Economy II*, US Department of Commerce, Jun 99, p3; also *Ev, p86 paragraph 2.3, p138 paragraph 19*

[39] Fletcher Research, press release 29 Jun 99

[40] And see *Q581*

[41] *Benchmarking* paragraph 2.10 and p18

—   250,000 firms had begun to use external communications technologies, such as the internet, electronic mail and EDI, regularly during the preceding year.[42] Firms representing 63% of the UK workforce — 600,000 in total — now use such technologies regularly, on a par with usage in most other G7 countries, except for France and Italy which lag some way behind

—   while large firms in the UK use external communications technologies as much as their international competitors, small and medium sized firms, particularly those with less than nine employees, perform relatively badly

—   firms representing only 9% of the UK workforce use their websites to sell goods, compared to 16% in Canada; 0.09% of UK retail sales currently occur over the internet, predicted to grow to 0.8% by 2001.

16. Separate reports were issued on the electronic commerce performance of different sectors of the UK economy, and of different regions.[43] These showed that:

—   technology-intensive manufacturing industries (such as chemicals and aerospace) and service industries (such as insurance) made far more use of external communications technologies than traditional business sectors (such as retailing and textiles). Traditional sectors were also more sceptical about the relevance of electronic commerce to their industries[44]

—   skills shortages emerged as a significant factor affecting firms wishing to develop their use of information and communications technologies

—   74% of London firms made regular use of external communications technologies, more than the average figure in any G7 country, but usage in the regions, particularly Northern Ireland and Wales, was much lower.

17. The international benchmarking exercises broadly bear out the Minister's comments to us that, in terms of the usage of information and communications technologies, the UK is "in the lead in Europe...[but] probably still somewhat behind the United States".[45] This assessment was shared by several witnesses and by many of the people we met in the United States, who perceived the UK as the best environment for electronic commerce in the EU.[46] The 1999 survey suggested that the UK has made some progress in narrowing the gap with the US and Canada but is now being challenged within Europe by Germany, perhaps due to recent telecommunications liberalisation there.[47] It must also not be forgotten that several countries beyond the G7 have wholeheartedly embraced new information and communications technologies, not least the Scandinavian nations, which lead the world in terms of mobile telephone usage, and Australia.[48]

18. **DTI are to be congratulated for the efforts they have made to ensure that the performance of UK businesses, in terms of information and communications technology usage, can be measured alongside that of other major economies. The results show that the UK is in a strong position to be at the forefront of the development of electronic commerce. There can be no room for complacency, however, and clear problems have been shown up. Very small businesses and some 'traditional' industrial sectors have not kept pace with their international competitors in this area and this may have a detrimental impact on the competitiveness of the UK economy in the years ahead. Government policy must focus on these firms and on those regions in which take-up of new information and communications technologies has been sluggish. The Regional Development Agencies and devolved bodies**

---

[42] See *Q587*

[43] *Moving into the Information Age: Sectoral Benchmarking Study*, DTI, Apr 99, URN99/798 and *Moving into the Information Age: Regional Benchmarking Study*, DTI, Apr 99, URN99/796

[44] Also see *e-manufacturing — harnessing the power of the web for manufacturing*, DTI, IBM and the Institute for Manufacturing, Apr 99

[45] *Q527*

[46] For the comments of witnesses see *Q50*; also see *Financial Times*, 23 Jun 99, p24

[47] see *Benchmarking* p5 and paragraph 1.3.1

[48] For instance see *The Emerging Digital Economy II*, US Department of Commerce, Jun 99, figure 1.2 shows that 35% of Scandinavian adults and 31% of Australian adults used the internet in 1998, compared to 37% of the US adult population but only 15% of adult Britons; the Australian Bureau of Statistics reported in July 1999 that 37% of adult Australians had used the internet during the twelve months prior to February 1999 (*Online Australia Update*, 5 Jul 99); on Scandinavia see *Ev, p222 paragraphs 34–5*

**may have an important role to play in this regard.**[49]

19. It is not altogether clear what the Government means by its aim for the UK to be the best environment for electronic trading by 2002. The Government has not defined the terms "environment" and "electronic trading" in this context and, as we noted above, the Minister wishes this to be one of the tasks of the e-Envoy, the appointment of which has still not been made. Although the Minister argued that 2002 was a "considerable time" away,[50] the clock is ticking and the Government's aim needs to be defined before the hour at which its achievement or otherwise must be judged is reached. DTI has indicated that it is considering using a basket of indicators to help assess the UK's environment for electronic trading.[51] It seems unlikely, however, that, by 2002, there will be proportionately more firms or individuals on-line in the UK than in the US; nor does it seem likely that the UK will lead the world in all, or even most, of the factors relating to electronic commerce identified by the Information Age Partnership. **Numerical indicators, for instance of the number of firms on-line, are not necessarily the best or only measures of the quality of the UK's environment for electronic trading. We suggest that the UK's legislative and regulatory framework, which the Information Age Partnership highlighted as an area of relative strength, should be taken into account when measuring the merits of that environment. The conclusions and recommendations we make in this Report, and those from our previous Report on electronic commerce, are intended to strengthen that framework and to help the Government achieve its ambitious aim for the UK to become the best environment for electronic trading by 2002.**

## II GOVERNMENT'S RESPONSE TO ELECTRONIC COMMERCE

20. From time to time new issues arise which require a policy response from Government. Examples in recent years include environmental concerns, particularly global warming, and the increasing use of drugs in society. In each case, the Government has had to identify specific ways in which it could usefully respond, as well as those areas in which Government intervention could have proved ineffective or deleterious. A further issue to consider in such circumstances is whether or not the existing structure of Government is best suited to deal with new problems, particularly those which cut across traditional departmental boundaries. Electronic commerce is an emerging issue which raises several new policy questions — for instance in relation to encryption, with which we recently dealt — and challenges existing policies — for instance, in relation to consumer protection and taxation. As with all new policy areas, the Government may be tempted into action in relation to almost every new issue associated with electronic commerce but many witnesses, calling for a "light regulatory touch", argued that the Government should not yield to such pressure.[52] **In considering how best to respond to the new challenges posed by electronic commerce, the Government must pay particular attention to those areas from which it should hold back from intervening.**

### Structure of Government

21. As a public policy issue, electronic commerce pays no respect to the departmental structures created by Government. The memorandum submitted to us by DTI included contributions from HM Treasury, the Inland Revenue, HM Customs and Excise, the Cabinet Office, the Home Office, the Department of Culture, Media and Sport, and the Department for Education and Employment.[53] Even this is by no means a definitive list of all those departments which might be concerned with electronic commerce. It will become increasingly difficult to identify a Government department or agency with no interest in or responsibility for some aspect of electronic commerce as the electronic Government agenda rolls-out. **Electronic commerce has the potential to change relationships within Government and between Government and society at large as well as to alter many public policy perspectives.**

22. We are concerned to ensure that Government is organised in such a way as to reflect and

---

[49] And see *Q179*

[50] *Q528*

[51] *Q527*

[52] *Qq98–9; Ev, p26 paragraph 2, p45 section 2.6, p50 section 8.8, p266 paragraph 9*

[53] *Ev, p193 paragraph 1.2*

cope with the cross-departmental nature of the issues raised by electronic commerce. At present, several parts of Government have responsibility for policy on electronic commerce, particularly:

— DTI, which is the lead department on electronic commerce and deals specifically with a number of issues, including encryption and authentication and the take-up of electronic commerce by small and medium sized enterprises, domestically and in international fora

— the Office of Telecommunications, which regulates prices for some telecommunication services, and oversees the development of telecommunications infrastructure

— the Inland Revenue and HM Customs and Excise, which are responsible for developing policy on the taxation of electronic commerce and appropriate customs charges

— the Cabinet Office, which is taking forward the electronic Government agenda

— the Department of Culture, Media and Sport, which is responsible for policy on internet content

— the Patent Office, which deals with intellectual property rights in the on-line environment.

23. There is, at present, no formal structure, such as a cabinet committee, to coordinate policy across these and other departments and agencies. The Prime Minister, on 10 December 1998, charged the Performance and Innovation Unit of the Cabinet Office, for which Lord Falconer of Thoroton has ministerial responsibility, with the task of establishing "how to achieve the Government's goal of making the UK the world's best environment for electronic commerce, ensuring that the UK benefits fully from the single fastest growing market place in the global economy".[54] It is expected to issue a report soon.[55] In addition, the then Secretary of State for Trade and Industry announced on 25 November 1998 the Government's intention to appoint a Special Representative on the Digital Economy for the UK (the e-Envoy) "to help to lead the United Kingdom in international discussions on electronic commerce".[56]

24. Governments abroad, faced with the same question of how best to tackle the issues thrown up by electronic commerce, have responded in a variety of ways. For instance, in:

— *Australia*, the Prime Minister announced in September 1997 the appointment of a Minister for Communications, the Information Economy and the Arts and the establishment of a Ministerial Council to help devise a "national strategy for the information economy". The National Office for the Information Economy was also set up, which, after a period of consultation, published Australia's "Strategic Framework for the Information Economy" in December 1998[57] and an assessment of progress to date in July 1999[58]

— *Canada*, the Government announced in September 1997 its target that Canada would be the "most connected nation in the world by 2000". A Task Force on Electronic Commerce was established within Industry Canada which formulated a wide-ranging electronic commerce strategy[59]

— *Denmark*, the Government appointed a committee in January 1999 to prepare a proposal for a new strategy entitled "Digital Denmark" by the end of the year[60]

— *Japan*, the Ministry of International Trade and Industry published an analysis of the policy challenges facing the Japanese Government in May 1997 and established the Electronic Commerce Promotion Council of Japan which has formed working groups covering a range of issues[61]

---

[54] HC Deb, 10 Dec 98, c278w; see HC Deb, 28 Jul 98, cc132–4w on the establishment of the Performance and Innovation Unit

[55] *Ev, p201 paragraph 7.2*

[56] HC Deb, 25 Nov 98, c217; *Ev, p202 paragraph 7.3*; and see paragraph 32

[57] *Building the Information Economy*, Jun 98, on the internet at www.noie.gov.au/docs/progrep.htm; *Report on the Consultation Process*, Nov 98, on the internet at www.noie.gov.au/docs/strategy/report1.html; and *A Strategic Framework for the Information Economy*, Dec 98, on the internet at www.noie.gov.au/strategy/document.html

[58] *A Strategic Framework for the Information Economy: Overview — key priorities for action*, National Office for the Information Economy, Jul 99 on the internet at www.noie.gov.au/strategy/strategic_summaries.htm

[59] The target was announced in the Speech from the Throne, 23 Sep 97; the electronic commerce strategy can be found on the internet at www.e-com.ic.gc.ca/english/60.html

[60] Details of the committee's remit can be found on the internet at /www.fsk.dk/cgi-bin/doc-show.cgi?doc_id=9794&doc_type=831&leftmenu=2

[61] See *Towards the Age of the Digital Economy*, MITI, May 97 and *ECOM Newsletter* #23, Mar 99, on the internet at www.ecom.or.jp/eng/kawara/23rd.html

— *New Zealand*, the Ministry of Commerce is developing a coordinated work programme on electronic commerce issues, drawing on the November 1998 strategy paper "Electronic Commerce: the Freezer Ship of the 21$^{st}$ Century"[62]

— the *United States*, a Presidential directive and framework for electronic commerce policy were issued in July 1997. The implementation of the directive is monitored by a Presidential working group which was established in 1995 and published a first annual report on electronic commerce policy in November 1998.[63] The President has also appointed a special advisor on electronic commerce policy, Ira Magaziner. The Department of Commerce has published two significant analyses of the emerging digital economy, the most recent in June 1999.[64]

25. None of our witnesses suggested that any of the policy areas relating to electronic commerce were, at present, misallocated within Government. We heard no calls for the creation of a Digital Unit or Division within a department such as DTI to be responsible for policy areas currently scattered across Whitehall. Nor did we receive evidence advocating the appointment of a Digital Minister, or in favour of nominating a Minister within each Department responsible for electronic commerce issues.[65] Several witnesses praised the strong role DTI had played in international fora during negotiations on electronic commerce issues but the Computing Services and Software Association questioned the extent to which Government policy on electronic commerce was coordinated or prioritised, especially compared to US policy.[66] **We do not think that the creation of a new unit or division within Government exclusively concerned with electronic commerce would be a useful innovation, or something welcomed by industry. Nor do we believe that it would necessarily be helpful at this stage to tinker with the division of responsibilities for electronic commerce policy between departments and agencies or to create new cross-departmental structures. Getting the policies right is more important.**

REGULATORY BODIES

26. Consumer organisations suggested to us that the convergence of communication technologies — including voice and data telecommunications and television — requires the establishment of a new communications regulator — OFCOM — replacing existing institutions, including OFTEL and the Independent Television Commission.[67] This mirrors the recent recommendation of the Culture, Media and Sport Committee that a variety of regulatory bodies be incorporated into a new Communications Regulation Commission.[68] The possibility of regulatory convergence being legislated for in order to deal more effectively with technological convergence was one option presented in the Government's July 1998 consultation paper on the regulation of communications.[69] In their follow-up to the consultation exercise, the Government confirmed that, in the short term at least, it foresaw closer collaboration between existing regulatory bodies rather than the creation of a new, consolidated agency as the way ahead.[70]

27. In practice, because connection to the internet almost invariably makes use of telecommunications networks, OFTEL has assumed regulatory responsibility for several significant aspects of electronic commerce.[71] As we will discuss later, OFTEL regulates the

---

[62] *Electronic Commerce: the Freezer Ship of the 21$^{st}$ Century*, New Zealand Ministry of Commerce, Nov 98, on the internet at www.moc.govt.nz/consumer/elcom/ecommerce/ecomm.html

[63] The Presidential framework is on the internet at www.ecommerce.gov/framewrk.htm; the Presidential directive can be found at www.ecommerce.gov/presiden.htm; the First Annual Report of the President's Working Group on Electronic Commerce can be located at www.doc.gov/ecommerce/E-comm.pdf; and see *Ev, pp224–5*

[64] The first report, *The Emerging Digital Economy*, was published by the US Department of Commerce in April 1998 and can be found on the internet at www.ecommerce.gov/emerging.htm; the second report, *The Emerging Digital Economy II*, was published in June 1999 and is on the internet at www.ecommerce.gov/ede/

[65] e centre$^{UK}$ called for a National Electronic Commerce Commission to be established to guide the e-Envoy — *Ev, p5 section 11*

[66] *Qq5, 54, 176*

[67] *Q223; Ev, pp264–5 section 5*

[68] Culture, Media and Sport Committee, Fourth Report, Session 1997/98, *The Multi-Media Revolution*, HC520-I, paragraph 158

[69] *Regulating Communications: approaching convergence in the information age*, DTI and DCMS, Jul 98, Cm4022, paragraphs 5.16–5.21

[70] *Regulating Communications: the way ahead*, DTI and DCMS, Jun 99, URN99/898

[71] *Ev, p135 paragraph 1*

charges made by some telecommunications operators for local calls to enable access to the internet and also monitors charges for high-bandwidth facilities such as ISDN and leased lines and the roll-out of high-bandwidth networks.[72] The Government has also proposed that OFTEL will run the accreditation scheme proposed for providers of encryption and authentication services.[73] Although other regulatory bodies — for instance, the Office of Fair Trading — will need to, and are, adapting to respond to the issues thrown up by electronic commerce, OFTEL has most work to do.

28. OFTEL has recently established a project to "identify OFTEL's role with respect to the emerging markets in electronic commerce and its regulation" which will include:[74]
— working with DTI on the Electronic Commerce Bill as it goes through Parliament to prepare for OFTEL's regulatory role in relation to electronic signature services
— working with DTI to influence the EU in the formulation and negotiation of legislation relating to electronic commerce with a view to ensuring the development of a coherent framework
— analysing the wider impact of the growth of electronic commerce and promoting recognition of key issues within OFTEL and in other Government departments.

**We note the work commenced by OFTEL to tackle the electronic commerce policy agenda, including issues well beyond those relating to authentication and encryption for which the Director General of Telecommunications might soon have statutory responsibility. OFTEL's electronic commerce team must quickly establish a cooperative relationship with the e-Envoy, when appointed, in order to ensure that their respective remits are appropriately coordinated.**

29. OFTEL's approach to policy issues is shaped by the duties and responsibilities placed on the Director General of Telecommunications, and the powers given to him, by the Telecommunications Act 1984. The Act was passed before the invention of the internet and before the rapid growth of electronic commerce began. Although data communications are implicitly covered by the duties, responsibilities and powers of the Director General, a more explicit recognition of the development of electronic commerce might now be desirable. An advantage of such a move might be to give issues relating to electronic commerce — such as the importance of unmetered local telephone calls and the more rapid roll-out of high-bandwidth telecommunications networks — more prominence within OFTEL and, as a result, within Government, perhaps through the appointment of a Director of Electronic Commerce, with a dedicated staff. Although we recognise that there has been some criticism of OFTEL's policies in relation to electronic commerce,[75] and a suggestion by BT that the regulation of telecommunications be reorganised,[76] we believe that there is a need for OFTEL to increase its focus on such issues. We are also concerned to ensure that work is undertaken to relate the concept of universal service, for which OFTEL is responsible in relation to telecommunications, to electronic commerce.[77] Furthermore, OFTEL's focus on competition, so that "customers...get the best possible deal in terms of quality, choice and value for money", might usefully be applied with more intensity to the host of firms now offering internet-related services.[78]

30. We are attracted by the option of a new duty on the Director General of Telecommunications in relation to electronic commerce because we judge that, at least for the short term, it reduces the need for new regulatory structures to be created to deal with electronic commerce. Although in the long term there may be a need for new structures, the Government's focus should now be on issues not institutions. Once electronic commerce policy initiatives are well underway, and future market trends have become clearer than is now the case, then attention should be turned to ensuring that the machinery of Government is designed to best reflect the needs of electronic commerce practitioners. For the time being, however, the Government's focus should be on ensuring that its electronic commerce policies fit the needs of industry and

---

[72] See paragraphs 40–65
[73] See *paragraphs 67–70*
[74] *Management Plan for 1999/2000*, OFTEL, May 1999, on the internet at/www.oftel.gov.uk/about/plan599.htm
[75] *Paragraph 69*
[76] *Ev, p61 section 8.11*
[77] Paragraph 77
[78] *Ev, p137 paragraph 15*

consumers.

31. DTI announced in the recent Competitiveness White Paper its intention to reform telecommunications regulation, taking account of responses to the consultation on convergence.[79] A Green Paper setting out options for reform is anticipated in November.[80] A Bill on utilities' regulation, including reform of OFTEL, is expected soon.[81] **We recommend that the Director General of Telecommunications be given a specific duty to facilitate electronic commerce, at the earliest opportunity. We would expect the Director General, in response, to publish a statement of how he intends to comply with his new duty.**

THE E-ENVOY

32. DTI published a job description for the e-Envoy on 3 December 1998.[82] It stated that the post-holder will:
— act as a public figurehead for the Government on electronic commerce issues in international discussions
— promote the UK as a centre for electronic commerce, business and investment
— publicly champion electronic commerce in the UK, spreading awareness and promoting up-take by businesses and consumers
— monitor progress on implementation of the electronic commerce strategy outlined in the recent Competitiveness White Paper and keep the strategy under regular and probing review
— review all existing Government policies and activities relating to electronic commerce, with a view to identifying gaps and areas for accelerated effort.

The e-Envoy will not be a civil servant. He will be a special adviser to the Secretary of State for Trade and Industry and, as required, to the Prime Minister. **Perceptions of the independence from Government of the e-Envoy are likely to be enhanced if it is made clear that the post-holder is not a civil servant.**

33. **We would welcome the appointment of an e-Envoy. The e-Envoy could be an effective ambassador for electronic commerce in the UK, an international ambassador for the UK as a centre of digital excellence and an advocate within Government for the policies and initiatives required for the UK to become the world's best environment for electronic trading. The appointment of a high-calibre, dynamic individual as e-Envoy could represent a high profile commitment by Government to electronic commerce, the like of which has so far been lacking.** The wide remit proposed for the e-Envoy's role, wider than the then Secretary of State indicated in his November statement, offers both opportunities and threats to the post-holder. On the one hand, with responsibility to oversee and influence policy on electronic commerce across Government and to promote that policy at home and abroad, the e-Envoy could become a key determinant of the direction electronic commerce policy takes and thereby have a significant, perhaps the most significant, influence on the success of that policy. On the other hand, if the relationships between the e-Envoy and Government Ministers and officials are not carefully defined and if the e-Envoy is denied the resources necessary for the job, then the post may become irrelevant and its holder sidelined.

34. **It is vital, therefore, that the Government, in consultation with the post-holder, devises and publishes the objectives of the e-Envoy and the resources which will be available to the e-Envoy to achieve those objectives.** Care must be taken to ensure that the e-Envoy's objectives are not so vague as to render impossible any assessment of their achievement. The job description used to advertise the post of e-Envoy in December 1998 might provide a useful basis upon which more specific objectives can be developed. **Progress made by the e-Envoy towards the achievement of his or her objectives should be assessed by means of measurable targets, drawn up by the Government. We would expect the e-Envoy to publish regular reports to Parliament detailing progress made towards the achievement of his or**

---

[79] *CWP*, paragraph 4.23

[80] *CWP Implementation Plan*, section D8

[81] HC Deb, 14 Apr 99, c263–7w

[82] *UK Special Representative on the Digital Economy (the e-Envoy): Information for Candidates*, DTI, Dec 98, on the internet at www.dti.gov.uk/e-Envoy/moreinfo.htm; and see HC Deb, 15 Mar 99, c476w

**her objectives, difficulties and obstacles met, and future targets set.**[83]

35.   It is unclear what resources, if any, the e-Envoy will have at his or her disposal. The e-Envoy will not possess statutory duties and powers nor a large staff to pursue his or her agenda, as might a regulator such as the Director General of Telecommunications. Nor is it likely that the e-Envoy will command a team of civil servants and others within DTI, akin to the e-commerce team in the Performance and Innovation Unit of the Cabinet Office, or the London Rough Sleepers Unit in the Department of the Environment, Transport and the Regions.[84] Unlike the UK Anti-Drugs Co-ordinator, it is not anticipated that the e-Envoy will have a deputy with which his or her workload can be shared.[85] It is important that the e-Envoy's objectives and targets reflect this limitation. In particular, **Ministers must not seek to burden the e-Envoy with a host of unduly ambitious and unrealistic objectives and responsibilities. The role of e-Envoy will be discredited if it is seen to combine responsibility without power. Ministers must define the policy framework within which the e-Envoy will work, rather than deflect difficult decisions and thorny issues towards a prominent but unempowered official.**

36.   The United Kingdom Anti-Drugs Co-ordinator has brought together a strategic steering group of senior officials from Government departments and agencies to implement the Government's drugs prevention and education agenda. We would anticipate the e-Envoy wishing to bring together a similar group of officials to co-ordinate Government policy on electronic commerce. The e-Envoy will report, in the first instance, to the Secretary of State for Trade and Industry, and, as a consequence, may be less able to take a broad, cross-departmental view of the relevant issues and to avoid inter-departmental rivalries and disputes than an official attached to the Cabinet Office. **In order to be effective, the e-Envoy must not be seen within Government as a DTI official, defending the department's line on issues which cut across departmental boundaries.**

37. On 26 May the Government announced its acceptance of the recommendations of the joint Government-industry team formed by the Cabinet Office's Performance and Innovation Unit, including that a new industry/Government forum be established to take forward discussion on encryption matters. It will be  chaired by a senior DTI official, with secretarial assistance provided by the Home Office.[86] Encryption is one the key cross-departmental policy issues relating to electronic commerce facing Government at the moment. **We see merit in the appointment of the proposed Government/industry forum and believe that it is essential that the e-Envoy participate in it.**

38. When DTI advertised the post of e-Envoy in December 1998, applications to fill it were requested to be submitted by 6 January 1999. Although that deadline has long since passed, the e-Envoy has not yet been appointed. The Government has responded to a succession of parliamentary questions on the subject by stating that an appointment will be made "shortly".[87] **The delay in appointing the e-Envoy, as yet unexplained, has not served to demonstrate the strength of the Government's commitment to the role or to the need for urgent policy initiatives on electronic commerce. It would seem to suggest, instead, that electronic commerce was not a priority of Government. We recommend that this impression be dispelled by an appointment at the earliest opportunity, so that the successful candidate can start making up for lost time.**

## III SOCIAL ISSUES

39. The internet is typically accessed by users in their homes and offices using a personal computer and an ordinary telephone line. Access to the internet is therefore restricted to those

---

[83] See *First Annual Report and National Plan*, United Kingdom Anti-Drugs Co-ordinator, Cabinet Office, 25 May 99

[84] DETR press release 162, 25 Feb 99

[85] Cabinet Office press notice 25/97, 14 Oct 97; First Annual Report on National Plan of the UK Anti–Drugs Co–ordinator, Cabinet Office, May 99 and see *Ev, p256 paragraph 5.6*

[86] *Encryption and Law Enforcement*, Performance and Innovation Unit, Cabinet Office, May 99, paragraphs 7.2–7.4

[87] For instance HC Deb 6 May 99 c449w, 18 May 99 c300w, 21 Jun 99 c313w

with the appropriate hardware, including a telephone connection,[88] and software, which can be expensive to acquire and maintain, and computer skills. There is a danger that those people without jobs which involve regular use of computers, without the means of buying the equipment needed to get onto the internet at home, or who are currently unable or unwilling to use computers may miss out on the benefits which it has been predicted electronic commerce might provide. The Government told us that one of its aims was to prevent the formation of a class of "information–have–nots" or "information poor", that is those people excluded from key aspects of the economy by their inability to use the internet, an objective with which we entirely agree.[89] We discuss below a number of policy debates which have arisen in relation to the possibility of an "information divide" developing in society.

### Internet Access

40. A number of witnesses raised with us issues relating to the *cost* of using the internet and the availability of telecommunications *infrastructure* by which the internet can be accessed, suggesting that, in both respects, UK users are comparatively worse off than their foreign, especially US, counterparts.[90] These issues are central to the Government's ambitions to permit more of its services to be available on-line and for the UK to become the best environment for electronic trading by 2002. Potential electronic commerce practitioners, particularly SMEs and consumers, will shy away from the internet if it is perceived to be slow, costly to use and prone to breakdown.

INFRASTRUCTURE

41. There are three principal means by which PC users may currently access the internet:

— by using a modem and a normal telephone line to "dial in". Modems convert information in digital form from a computer into analogue form, and vice versa, enabling a standard telephone line to be used for electronic communications. Modems provide low bandwidth access, typically at most 56Kbit/s.[91] It can take several minutes for a large file, piece of software, sound or video clip to be downloaded onto a computer by a modem

— by using an integrated services digital network (ISDN), which allows users to communicate in digital form, by-passing the analogue network. ISDN can utilise the 64Kbit/s bandwidth of the digital public telecommunications network to the full. ISDN2 can provide 128Kbit/s bandwidth, by allowing two channels of communication to be opened simultaneously[92]

— by using leased lines which provide permanent point-to-point communication links dedicated to the customer's exclusive use. Leased lines are available at a range of bandwidths, from 65kbit/s to upwards of 2Mbit/s.[93]

Higher bandwidth services tend to cost more to set up than lower bandwidth services. Consequently, leased lines tend to be used by business customers, especially those offering on-line services; ISDN by SMEs and some residential users; and modems by residential users.[94] Few residential users and SMEs access the internet by means of high-bandwidth facilities, such as leased lines.

42. The Government told us that "the UK is already one of the most liberalised telecommunications markets in the World" and we have already noted that the business-led Information Age Partnership described the UK's telecommunications infrastructure as a source of competitive advantage.[95] A recent report by the US Government commented that the UK had "one of the most liberalised telecommunications markets in Europe" and that "UK companies are using innovations in pricing and content to offset some of the advantages that US companies

---

[88]The National Council Consumer reported that 7% of UK households do not have a telephone connection — *Ev, p86 paragraph 2.4*

[89] *Ev, p200 paragraph 5.2*; see also *Ev, p90 paragraph 7.4, p263*

[90] *Ev, p111 section 9*

[91] Bandwidth is the physical characteristic of a telecommunications system that indicates the speed at which information can be transferred, measured in digital systems in kilobytes per second (Kbit/s) or megabytes per second (Mbit/s)

[92] See *Ev, p50 section 8.7*

[93] For definitions see OFTEL's web site at www.oftel.gov.uk/glossary.htm and *Ev, pp140–1 paragraphs 42, 47–8*

[94] *Ev, pp140–1 paragraphs 42, 47*

[95] *Ev, p195 paragraph 4.4*; also *Qq123, 585*; *Ev, p266 paragraph 11*; and see paragraph 14

gained by being early into the UK markets" as a result.[96] The CBI emphasised the need for increased telecommunications liberalisation in Europe in order to improve EU competitiveness in relation to the US.[97] Although telecommunications liberalisation has advanced further in the UK than in several other European countries, we outline below some of the significant problems that remain.

*The Local Loop*

43. In 1994 our predecessor Committee reported on the UK's high-bandwidth, or broadband, communications network, focussing on "the importance of Britain developing a national optical fibre network extending to individual homes and businesses".[98] The Committee identified a number of benefits which might result from the establishment of such a network including in relation to the UK's economic competitiveness and improvements in public service.[99] Witnesses argued that the UK stood to take advantage of similar benefits from the extension of high-bandwidth networks. The CBI, for instance, told us that "easy access to high-speed digital telecommunications, at reasonable cost, is essential" if the aims of the Government's competitiveness agenda are to be achieved.[100]

44. We asked OFTEL why, since 1994, high-bandwidth networks had not been extensively rolled-out to residential and small business users. Mr Walker, Director Technology, OFTEL, explained that telecommunications firms had not generally planned to extend fibre optic networks to residential users and SMEs because of the cost of doing so, but that new Digital Subscriber Loop (DSL) technologies had now "radically changed the opinions of the telecoms industry towards what was seen as the obsolescent copper network" which were now regarded as "potentially the vehicle for delivering high-bandwidth services to a much wider range of customers" than was previously foreseen.[101] Such technologies are being commercially deployed overseas and are being trialed in the UK.[102] Other new technologies, including third-generation mobile telephones, cable modems and satellite telephones might also permit widespread high-bandwidth internet access in future.[103]

45. The Campaign for Unmetered Telecommunications (CUT) unfavourably compared the rate at which DSL and other new high-bandwidth technologies are being rolled-out in the UK with the pace of change in other European countries and the US.[104] BT rejected such a comparison, arguing that "in terms of upgrading the speed of these local copper loops...we are not significantly behind anywhere else."[105] Nevertheless, OFTEL published in December 1998 a consultation document seeking views on the likely future demand for high-bandwidth services, whether that demand is being adequately met, and, if barriers to that demand being satisfied exist, how they can be reduced.[106] OFTEL told us that it was examining "whether we believe BT will rise to the challenge not only of providing the services they choose to supply over the network, but also providing the wholesale services to other operators and service providers so that they too can enter that market."[107] OFTEL published its conclusions on access to the local loop on 6 July 1999. It concluded that "there is unmet demand in the SME sector for higher bandwidth services" and that, consequently, BT's competitors should be able to upgrade BT's local telephone lines in order to provide their own high-bandwidth services to consumers and that, when BT upgrades its network, access to the upgraded lines should be available on a fair

---

[96] *The Emerging Digital Economy II*, US Department of Commerce, Jun 99, p8
[97] *Q71* and *Ev, p28 paragraph 16*; also *Q125*
[98] Trade and Industry Committee, Third Report, Session 1993/94, *Optical Fibre Networks*, HC285–I; quotation from paragraph 3; also see HC285–iv Qq343–8; and *Q126*
[99] *Ibid*, paragraphs 12–17
[100] *Ev, p28 paragraph 16*
[101] *Qq405–6*; *Ev p143 paragraphs 68, 70*; and see *Q126*
[102] Ev, p19 paragraph 31; *Qq123, 408*; *Ev, p50 section 8.7, p313 paragraphs 5.1–5.8*. In the US we heard from the Mayor of Palo Alto, California, of the ambitious programme being undertaken by the local authority there to lay optical fibre cables to each household and business in the district
[103] See paragraph 48
[104] *Ev, p313 paragraphs 5.1–5.8*; also *Ev, p255 paragraph 3.5, p293 question 2*
[105] *Qq123, 126*
[106] *Q408*; *Access to Bandwidth*, OFTEL, Dec 98, which can be found on the internet at www.oftel.gov.uk/competition/llu1298.htm
[107] *Q414*

basis.[108]

46. DSL technologies are only one means of providing high-bandwidth services; ISDN and leased lines may be more appropriate for business users; cable modems are beginning to be rolled-out; and interactive television may offer non-PC high-bandwidth services to a significant proportion of residential consumers.[109] **We agree with OFTEL, however, that BT's monopoly ownership and control of the local loop could restrict the roll-out of vital new high-bandwidth services. Although OFTEL has no role to play in championing the development of particular technologies — such as DSL — we believe that it must be proactive in ensuring that competitive forces exert their influence throughout the UK's telecommunications infrastructure so that residential consumers and small and medium sized enterprises can benefit from a choice of high-bandwidth technologies from different operators.**

*ISDN*

47. ISDN is only available to those consumers located within a short distance — around three to five kilometres — of a telephone exchange.[110] The Federation of Small Businesses warned that this caused a "reduction in the value of electronic communication in rural areas" which put such areas at "a major disadvantage".[111] BT told us that this limitation to their services would continue to exist for "some time", although local exchanges are gradually being improved.[112] A similar limitation is likely to affect DSL technologies.[113] **Electronic commerce offers the opportunity to unlock the potential of the rural economy. The Government must ensure that this opportunity is exploited, not wasted due to deficiencies in the nation's telecommunications infrastructure, by ensuring that there exists effective competition in the supply of high-bandwidth services to all users, not just those in urban or suburban areas.**

*Alternative Delivery Mechanisms*

48. Witnesses mentioned a number of emerging alternative means by which the internet could be accessed, and electronic commerce carried out in future, including:

— interactive television, building on the recent commencement of digital television services, which has the potential to provide a low-tech means of internet access to people without computer equipment or skills[114]

— other fixed cable networks, including broadband access using the cable television network and the electricity supply network[115]

— third generation mobile telephones, the radio spectrum for which is planned to be auctioned by the Government in the second half of 1999/2000[116]

— other wireless mechanisms, include radio-based and satellite systems.[117]

It is not possible to say which, if any, of these possibilities will become prevalent in the next century; in what situations they might replace the PC as the usual means of providing access to the internet; or to anticipate the development of any further, as yet unexplored, possible means of linking computers and computer networks. Interactive television is predicted to be the most advanced of these technologies, although all might be commercially available within five to ten years.[118] OFTEL must, however, be mindful of the need to ensure that there are no market

---

[108] *Access to Bandwidth: Proposals for Action*, OFTEL, Jul 99, especially p2 and chapter 5; also OFTEL press notice 41/99, 6 Jul 99; but see *Qq123–5* for BT's views on local loop unbundling (prior to the release of OFTEL's July 1999 *Proposals for Action*) and *The Times*, 7 Jul 99 for BT's reaction to OFTEL's conclusions

[109] See paragraph 48

[110] *Qq 39, 121*; OFTEL has published an on-line guide to ISDN availability at www.oftel.gov.uk/consumer/smallbus/sbtf499.htm

[111] *Q78*

[112] *Qq121–2*

[113] *Q417*

[114] *Qq71, 192–3, 465; Ev, p50 section 8.4, p221 paragraph 32, p249 paragraph 13, p261, p266 paragraph 24*

[115] For cable modems see *Ev, p143 paragraph 69*; for the electricity network see *Daily Telegraph*, 16 Mar 99, p29

[116] *Ev, p10 paragraph 4; Q39; Ev, p50 section 8.7*; on the auctions see DTI press noticse 99/378, 6 May 99; 99/549, 23 Jun 99

[117] For instance, see the memorandum we received from Tele2 (UK) — *Ev, pp301-2*; also Ev, p19 paragraph 32; DTI Press notice 99/581, 5 Jul 99, on the launch of the consultation exercise *Wireless in the Information Age* which can be found on the internet at www.open.gov.uk/radiocom/broadband/intro.htm

[118] For instance see *The Times*, Interface section, 30 Sep 98, p8; *Sunday Business*, 15 Nov 98, p28; *Independent*, 11 Feb 99, p10; *Financial Times*, 18 May 99, p18; *Financial Times*, 22 Jun 99, p34

barriers to the development and take-up of these technologies; and the Government should seek to ensure that British industry is at the crest of this technological wave.

COST

49. The debate about the cost of using the internet encompasses several different issues:-
— the charges made by internet service providers
— the cost of local telephone calls
— charges for high-bandwidth services
— prices of computer hardware.
Each has been the source of recent controversy, with the suggestion made in each case that UK users pay more to access the internet than their counterparts overseas.

*ISP Charges*

50. A recent study of the charges made by internet service providers (ISPs) — often a monthly flat-rate fee — additional to the telecommunications cost of internet use suggested that such charges were higher in the UK than in Europe and the US.[119] The Internet Service Providers' Association described the analysis as "fairly simplistic" particularly in the light of changes to the UK's ISP market since late 1998, including the emergence of around 150 ISPs which do not make access charges.[120] "Free" ISPs have proved popular with consumers.[121] OFTEL told us that, with 300 internet service providers operating in the UK, there exists a "fairly competitive market" but the possibility exists of market distortions being caused by firms cross-subsidising their ISP operations from revenues earned elsewhere.[122] The Internet Service Providers' Association cautioned against undue regulation of the market because of its dynamic nature, a point which was reiterated on several occasions by electronic commerce practitioners during our visit to the United States.[123] OFTEL has already begun to deal with issues raised by "free" ISPs, including the division of revenues from calls made to ISPs between the telecommunications operator and the receiving firm, and have undertaken to keep under review the cross-subsidisation issue.[124]

*Local Telephone Calls*

51. Most consumers accessing the internet by means of a modem and an ordinary telephone line do so by dialling their ISP's locally-charged (eg 0845) telephone number.[125] **For most residential customers and SMEs using the internet, local telephone charges are the marginal cost of going on-line and, as such, are a key influence over the extent to which such consumers and enterprises engage in electronic commerce.** Several witnesses complained that the cost of local telephone calls was a serious barrier to electronic commerce, particularly when compared to the US where consumers in most States can choose unmetered local calls.[126] A recent US Government report stated that "a factor facilitating e-commerce growth in the United States is the flat rate pricing structure of local residential telephone calls...The pricing structures in most other countries are not so conducive to online shopping".[127] One of the witnesses we received evidence from, the Campaign for Unmetered Telecommunications, was established to focus on "dissatisfaction about the cost of accessing the internet from home in the UK".[128]

52. It could be said that there is no such thing as cost-free internet access. Where US customers can take advantage of unmetered local telephone calls, they often pay a higher line rental fee than would otherwise be the case. Even if customers were offered internet access

[119] See *Financial Times*, 11 Jan 99
[120] Ev, p16 paragraph 8
[121] *Q395*
[122] *Q394*
[123] *Qq198–9*; also *Ev, p139 paragraph 26*
[124] Ev, p17 paragraphs 13–17; *Qq396, 398*; *Ev, p138 paragraphs 22–4*; *OFTEL Consultation Paper on the Relationship between Retail Prices and Interconnection Charges for Number Translation Services*, Mar 99 and OFTEL press notice 14/99, 10 Mar 99
[125] Some ISPs now offer free 0800 access to the internet at certain times — for instance see *Independent*, 7 Jun 99, p12
[126] *Qq34, 245–6*; *Ev, p154 section 6, p255 paragraph 3.3, p296 paragraph 1, p298 paragraph 12*; for BT's comments on the US position see *Ev, p64*
[127] *The Emerging Digital Economy II*, US Department of Commerce, p7
[128] *Ev, p309 paragraph 1.5*

without being required to pay the service provider or telecommunications firm, the service would still be paid for out of revenues earned from other activities —long distance telephone calls, for instance.[129]

53. Data on telecommunications prices and costs is notoriously hard to come by, rendering international comparisons difficult at best. OFTEL warned us that price comparisons with the US were complicated by differences between States because much telecoms regulation is based at State level.[130] The Director General of Telecommunications told us recently that, in the UK, "the tariff material provided by the telephone companies is actually confusing for the consumer. I think it is very difficult to work out who you get the best buy from...I want to see if we can produce something that is much clearer and much simpler".[131] **We welcome OFTEL's recognition that consumers need full and clear information about the tariffs charged by different telephone operators in order for them to take full advantage of the opportunities offered by competition in the telecommunications market. Urgent progress in this area is now required.**

54. Despite the difficulties involved with comparing telephone tariffs between companies and internationally, the OECD has recently undertaken an analysis which suggests that BT's charges for local telephone calls are competitive within Europe, although perhaps less so with the US. OFTEL argued to us that a UK customer taking advantage of a free internet service provider and a cable telephone operator would already benefit from some of the lowest charges for internet use in the OECD, especially for off-peak connections.[132] OFTEL is undertaking "further internal research on various aspects of the cost of using the internet and supplying internet access in the UK compared with other countries" which we look forward to seeing.[133]

55. OFTEL told us that "we are not against free local calls as a point of principle" but that such calls must not be subsidised by other aspects of the service provider's business.[134] It indicated that "free" internet access in the US had been paid for, at least in part, by higher tariffs for long distance calls.[135] CUT disputed this point, arguing that "prices for long-distance and international calls from most US operators are roughly comparable to BT's" and that, because of the structure of the US telecommunications market, direct cross-subsidy from national and international calls to local calls was "improbable if not impossible".[136] Thomas Long, an American visiting fellow at Glasgow University, provided us with a comparison of telecommunications charges between California and the UK and concluded that "even with most of its residential customers taking unmetered local service, Pacific Bell is able to offer a substantially better deal for local services than BT, while offering a broadly comparable deal for long distance calls."[137]

56. OFTEL also raised concerns about the impact unmetered telephone calls might have on the telecommunications network.[138] Unmetered calling might not provide an incentive for customers to log off the internet, increasing usage of the network and possibly causing congestion. OFTEL stated that there were instances in the US of calls to emergency services not being connected because of network congestion.[139] CUT, citing data prepared by internet service provider America On-Line, stated that the average duration of internet sessions in the US was 55 minutes, "not infinitely long", compared to 16 minutes in the UK. They also noted that it was

---

[129] *Qq 106–8, 111*

[130] Ev, p18 paragraph 20

[131] Trade and Industry Committee, Fifth Report, Session 1998/99, *Telephone Numbering*, HC139, Q74 and also Qq73, 75–81

[132] Ev, p18 paragraph 22; *Ev, p139 paragraphs 27–31, pp144-45*; also see *Qq106, 399*

[133] Ev, pp17–18 paragraph 19

[134] *Q399*

[135] Ev, p18 paragraph 21; *Ev, p139 paragraph 33*; and *Q111; Ev, p266 paragraph 12*

[136] *Ev, p314 paragraphs 6.3.2–6.3.3*

[137] Ev, p9; also see *Ev, pp318–9 Annex 2*

[138] Ev, p18 paragraph 25

[139] *Ev, p139 paragraph 36*; also *Q400; Ev, p266 paragraph 13.* We asked for more information about this from OFTEL — see Ev, pp19–20 paragraphs 33–37. The US information cited by OFTEL included an article in the *Seattle Times*, 23 Jan 98, on the internet at www.seattletimes.com/news/business/html98/fone_012398.html and New Hampshire Public Utilities Commission Order of Notice DT99–020, on the internet at www.puc.state.nh.us/99020ont.html

possible for ISPs to set a maximum limit to the duration of internet calls.[140] Mr Long claimed to be unaware of any examples of calls to emergency services failing to be connected because of network congestion in the US and told us that "in California, the state with the highest concentration of internet users, there is absolutely no problem completing calls of any type at any time of day or night."[141]

57. Another issue raised by OFTEL was that unmetered local calling might fail to provide adequate incentives for investment in the local telecommunications network, while at the same time increasing the need for such investment to be made.[142] Again, arguments were advanced in opposition to OFTEL's suggestion. Mr. Long said that "additional local calling stimulates demand for additional phone lines...additional lines is an area of fast growth for US local operators."[143] CUT questioned whether additional infrastructural investment would be required as a result of unmetered local calling given current patterns of internet usage and also argued that congestion "sparks off technical advances in telecommunications hardware and software".[144] OFTEL themselves gave us examples of innovations in the utilisation of the public telecommunications network in response to increased internet usage.[145]

58. Operators are increasingly responding to the apparent demand for unmetered or free local telephone calls for internet use.[146] Recent press reports have suggested that BT is negotiating with OFTEL a new tariff package including unmetered local calling.[147] OFTEL must clearly be vigilant in ensuring that such packages are fair,[148] and do not discriminate against consumers who wish to retain metered calling, but we welcome the trend towards unmetered local calling. **The possibility of receiving a substantial telephone bill as a result of regular use of the internet, and the widespread perception of this occurring, seem to us to be obvious disincentives to greater use of the internet and, therefore, participation in electronic commerce.**[149] Although BT claimed that there was little or no correlation between internet usage and the price of local telephone calls, this evidence was directly contradicted by many of the business people, policy makers and opinion formers we met with in the United States.[150]

59. **The more widespread availability to residential customers of unmetered local telephone calls would give electronic commerce in the UK a substantial boost.** Although there may be disadvantages to unmetered local calls, these pale into insignificance when examined alongside the potential benefits. As one senior US businessman told us on our recent visit, "you would not charge people by the second to browse in a shop; so why should we accept that customers be charged in that way for visiting websites of interest?" OFTEL can not, and should not, mandate specific tariff options but they can encourage beneficial developments, including by providing customers with the comparative tariff data required to facilitate informed choices.[151] **We judge that OFTEL has been unduly cautious in emphasising the possible disadvantages of unmetered local calls, at the expense of the potential benefits. In line with our recommendation that the Director General of Telecommunication be given a duty to facilitate electronic commerce,[152] we recommend that OFTEL investigates what, if any, regulatory actions are required to encourage innovative tariff packages being offered to internet users throughout the UK; and devote resources to studying and publicising the comparative costs of internet access packages, in order to dispel the seemingly widespread perception that anything more than a cursory use of the internet would prove prohibitively expensive.**

---

[140] *Ev, p316 paragraphs 6.8.5–6.8.6*
[141] Ev, p8
[142] Ev, p18 paragraph 26; *Ev, p140 paragraphs 35, 37*
[143] Ev, p8
[144] *Ev, p315 section 6.7*
[145] Ev, p19 paragraph 30
[146] *Ev, p140 paragraphs 39–40*; and see Ev, p16 paragraph 9
[147] *Sunday Telegraph*, 23 May 99, *Guardian*, 24 May 99, but see *Qq106–11*
[148] See Ev, pp16–17 paragraphs 10–11
[149] *Q91*; *Ev, p249 paragraph 15*; for BT's evidence about consumers' perceptions of telecommunications costs see *Qq144–5*; *Ev, p64*
[150] For BT's claim see *Qq106–7, 113*; for arguments in support of a correlation see *Q189*; *Ev, p75 section 5.i*
[151] See paragraph 53
[152] See paragraph 31

*ISDN and Leased Lines*

60. Several witnesses complained about the costs of ISDN and leased lines in the UK and in Europe, relative to the US, and concluded that there had been inadequate regulation of these aspects of the telecommunications market.[153] The Telecommunication Managers' Association stated that "there is no effective competition in the UK to BT's Basic Rate ISDN2 access and we are again one of the most expensive countries in Europe...OFTEL refuses to examine BT's high start-up costs for the service and other providers are content to cruise under BT's (unregulated) price umbrella, thus forming what appears to be an effective complex monopoly".[154] The Internet Service Providers' Association told us that "European costs for leased circuits are significantly higher than in the USA. It is an area where the regulatory environment for telecommunications seems to have failed us. These costs are a significant direct or indirect burden for all UK industry wishing to use the internet for commerce".[155]

61. Recent surveys of prices for ISDN and leased lines in the UK and elsewhere have served to substantiate the complaints made about the prices of such facilities. A survey of BT's charges for basic connection and rental for ISDN packages suggested that UK customers pay up to six times as much for this service as customers elsewhere in Europe.[156] Representations were made to OFTEL in late 1997 that the prices for long-distance 2Mbt/s leased lines were 50% cheaper in the US, 66% cheaper in Sweden and 10% cheaper in Germany than those charged in the UK by BT.[157] The Telecommunications' Managers Association told us that "the cost of a cross-border leased line in Europe can be as much as 16 times the price of an equivalent leased line in the USA."[158] We pressed BT in oral evidence on the prices they charge for leased lines, which the Internet Service Providers' Association had described as "the backbone of the internet".[159] Sir Peter Bonfield argued that "by and large, what we have here is not significantly different from the United States. There might be some areas where we are more or less expensive, but certainly the price has come down on leased circuits".[160]

62. In relation to ISDN, OFTEL told us that there were now 20 firms offering the service and that "on average most businesses in urban areas now have access to at least two operators' services". It cited a survey by OVUM, which focused on large businesses, and which found that UK call and rental (not connection) charges for ISDN services were slightly above the EU average but well below US charges. OFTEL informed us that it was "continuing to closely monitor the development of the ISDN market".[161]

63. OFTEL launched an investigation into UK prices for leased lines in December 1997 which reported in January 1999. OFTEL concluded that "UK prices are not significantly higher than those in other countries" and that "a combination of existing price caps and increasing competition are reducing UK prices for leased lines". It found that competition between providers of leased lines was particularly strong in central London and that unpublished discounts, particularly to large firms leasing long-distance lines in the US, were a significant influence on comparisons of European and US prices.[162] Although OFTEL proposed two reforms to "ensure that competition continues to develop and to place downward pressure on UK prices", users of leased lines remain dissatisfied.[163] The Internet Service Providers' Association, for instance, argued that "comparing UK costs to expensive European ones and being satisfied that they are 'not significantly above' is clearly not in keeping with the Government's ambitions for

---

[153] For instance *Qq71, 189*

[154] *Ev, p238*

[155] *Ev, p82 section 4* and *p292 question 2*

[156] *Financial Times*, 15 Sep 98; and see *Ev, p312 paragraph 4.8*

[157] *Ev, p139 paragraph 51*

[158] *Ev, p238*

[159] *Ibid*

[160] *Q119*

[161] *Ev, pp140–1 paragraphs 43–6*

[162] *Ev, pp141–2 paragraphs 47–65*; also *Q401* and National *Leased Lines in the UK: summary of OFTEL's investigation*, OFTEL, Jan 99

[163] *Ev, p142 paragraph 65*; *Competition Bulletin*, OFTEL, #12 Apr 99, section "Other Compliance Issues"

the UK in the field of e-commerce."[164]

64. OFTEL intends to study further the relative prices of leased lines in the UK and the US and the extent to which there exists competition between providers of leased lines in the UK, particularly outside of central London.[165] We welcome this commitment but would suggest that a thorough, more wide-ranging analysis of the competitiveness of the UK markets for high-bandwidth services, including ISDN as well as leased lines, is needed. **Without high-bandwidth services, in particular leased lines, UK businesses will be unable to offer effective and innovative electronic services, resulting in their competitive advantages being ceded to foreign rivals. Ensuring that UK firms have a choice of competitively-priced high-quality high-bandwidth services must be an urgent priority for OFTEL.**

65. As the Internet Service Providers' Association identified, although the prices of UK leased lines may be competitive in European terms, they are less competitive when compared to the prices charged in the US. This is an issue which must be tackled at European level. DTI told us that it had "raised the issue of cost of leased lines in Europe with the European Commission in a number of fora" and had encouraged the Commission to undertake a speedy examination of European leased line prices, with a view to assessing the need to strengthen the provisions of the Leased Lines Directive.[166] **We support the Government in its efforts to focus the attention of the European Commission on the need to ensure that European leased lines prices are competitive with those offered in the US.**

*Hardware*
66. The Government recently reported that prices of personal computers, the primary means by which the internet is accessed at present, are higher in the UK than in the US, Japan, France and Germany.[167] Cable & Wireless Communications described hardware prices as "the most significant cost barrier to e–commerce for consumers".[168] This is something which the Government's forthcoming assessment of international price comparisons might usefully consider in more depth.[169] We are also concerned that, due to rapid technological developments, computer hardware can suffer from an "almost built-in obsolescence" which may require consumers to spend substantial sums of money simply to keep pace with the latest capabilities — such as the internet — and software.[170] **We welcome the work being undertaken by DTI to compare the prices of consumer goods in the UK and elsewhere and hope that it will be followed by swift action to ensure that British consumers fully benefit from competition in the computer hardware market.**

**Payment on the Internet**
67. At present, the standard means by which consumers pay for goods on the internet is by credit card.[171] Those consumers without a bank account, or who have chosen not to hold a credit card, or who have been refused a credit card for some reason, are effectively excluded from involvement with electronic commerce.[172] The National Consumer Council told us that only 36% of UK adults use credit cards.[173] Internet users may be reluctant to pay for goods on-line with credit cards because of fears about the security of such transactions.[174] Alternative means of paying for goods and services on-line are being brought forward, which, as well as catering for the concerns already noted, could facilitate small on-line payments which are not usually

---

[164] *Ev, p293 section 2*; also see *Ev, p238*

[165] *Competition Bulletin*, OFTEL, #12 Apr 99, section "Other Compliance Issues"; and *Q402*

[166] Ev, p5 question 10

[167] *Competitiveness White Paper: Benchmarking the Digital Economy*, DTI, Dec 98, URN98/1037, appendix section 2; and see *Financial Times* 19 Nov 98, 20 Nov 98, 15 Jan 99 and *Daily Telegraph* 24 Nov 98; also *Qq164–5, 168–74*

[168] *Ev, p266 paragraph 14*

[169] See DTI Press notice 99/223, 10 Mar 99; HC Deb, 17 Jun 99, c554

[170] *Qq166–7, 244*; and a related point *Ev, p327 paragraph 3.3*

[171] Business–business payments often make use of dedicated closed networks — see *Ev, p3 section 6, pp10–1 annex 4, p107 section 4, pp111–5 annex A, p223 paragraph 43*

[172] *Ev, p154 section 7*

[173] *Ev, p86 paragraph 2.4.* A recent report by the Joseph Rowntree Foundation showed that 1.5 million households did not have access to bank accounts — see BBC *Online*, "1.5 million lack access to financial services", 22 Mar 99

[174] For instance *Qq85, 285*

allowed to be made by credit card.[175] APACS told us about the development of on-line debit cards, which might be of benefit to consumers who have bank accounts but not credit cards.[176] There have also been several UK trials of electronic cash schemes, for instance whereby consumers charge cards with often small amounts of money and use them to make on-line purchases.[177]

68. There are problems associated with the widespread adoption of new payment methods for on-line transactions. The Government told us that "the lack of universally-agreed standards may slow the development of electronic money as an alternative payment system" and that the effects of such systems on "prudent monetary policy [and] the potential for fraud, tax evasion [and] money laundering" were all of concern.[178] The law enforcement agencies submitted to us a paper on the effects increased usage of electronic money might have on their policies to combat money laundering.[179] Many of these issues were the subject of a recent report by the European Central Bank and the European Commission has issued draft directives on the harmonisation of electronic money schemes across Europe.[180]

69. The legislative proposals made by the European Commission, and the issues raised by the European Central Bank, are primarily concerned with the extent to which electronic money, and the firms which issue it, should be subject to banking rules and regulations. While this is undoubtedly an important question to consider, we think that there should also be a focus on ensuring that all sectors of society can participate in electronic commerce.[181] The Government told us that the Electronic Commerce Bill would make the use of electronic money easier through the gradual adoption of smart cards,[182] but barriers to their use by disadvantaged members of society might remain. **The Government should examine how consumers without bank accounts can be encouraged to participate in electronic commerce.**

### Skills

70. In recent years, consumers throughout society have become accustomed to using reasonably complex technology — mobile telephones, satellite television and automated cash machines, for instance. These technologies are relatively user-friendly: although they make use of recent technological advances, they do so in ways which are unobtrusive. Their users make simple, familiar choices, which are quickly effected by hardware and software behind the scenes. Use of the internet is generally far less easy, requiring a personal computer, choice of a software package, and then at least some understanding of how the information required can be found, how unwanted information can be avoided, how links between pages work and of the jargon which litters websites. The internet is a hostile environment for anyone unfamiliar with a personal computer, particularly given the prevalence of anecdotes about its perils — including poor security, limited data protection and the ease with which pornography can be encountered.[183] **Participation in electronic commerce requires more than computer hardware and software and an appropriate connection to the telecommunications network; skills, and the confidence to deploy those skills, are essential.**

71. Electronic commerce could be made more user-friendly. Electronic mail, although requiring a personal computer, is far simpler to use than the internet. Internet access via television sets or mobile telephones might help attract users previously deterred by the thought of needing to master a computer. The mechanisms of electronic Government could, and should, be very simple to operate. Internet service providers are increasingly developing their own

---

[175] For instance see *Qq285–6,308, 310–12*; *Ev, p51 section 9.3*

[176] *Q309*

[177] For instance see *Ev, p199 paragraph 4.42*

[178] *Ev, p199 paragraph 4.43*

[179] *Ev, pp126–7 Annex A*; and *Qq373–8*

[180] *Ev, p199 paragraph 4.46*; *Report on Electronic Money*, European Central Bank, Aug 98; proposals for directives on the coordination of laws, regulations and administrative provisions relating to the taking up and pursuit of the business of credit institutions; and on the taking up, the pursuit, and the prudential supervision of the business of electronic money institutions, 29 Jul 98, Com(461)98 and (for criticism of the draft Directives see *Ev, p51 section 9.4*); European Legislation Committee, Fortieth Report, 1997/98, HC155-xl, ppvii–ix

[181] *Qq241–3*

[182] *Ev, p199 paragraph 4.45*

[183] *Ev, p262*

websites into "contents pages" for the internet, which facilitate swift access to popular resources, such as on-line encyclopaedias, travel information and shopping sites.[184] Nevertheless, for as long as electronic commerce primarily involves the internet, accessed by means of a personal computer, then potential users with limited computer skills will avoid it.

72. The Government has focused on making computers available in schools and public places such as libraries in order to encourage access to the internet and related on-line resources.[185] While not wishing to detract from this strategy, the provision of equipment and appropriate software must be matched by training for those staff, including teachers and librarians, who will help potential users go on-line for the first time. Anyone trying to use the internet for the first time without adequate help and advice is almost bound to find the experience underwhelming, perhaps to the extent that future use of the internet is discouraged. This issue is of particular relevance to schools, given that the Government aims for all school leavers to be "competent using digital technologies" by 2002.[186] The Department for Education and Employment (DfEE) recently estimated that some 30 per cent of primary schools and 90 per cent of secondary schools in England currently have some form of internet access, but these facilities might not all be well used.[187] Further data from DfEE has shown that only 65% of primary school teachers and 61% of secondary school teachers felt confident in the use of information technology within the curriculum.[188] **This would suggest the possibility of a gap between the provision of internet access in schools and the ability of teachers to make use of that access, once provided.**

73. The Government has indicated that a key priority is ensuring that owners of small and medium sized enterprises have the skills necessary to exploit electronic commerce. e centre[UK] told us that "UK competitiveness is held back because of the lack of readily available knowledge amongst...business advisors".[189] DTI is backing the Advisor Skills Initiative, piloted by BT, Compaq and Microsoft, which aims to ensure that small business advisors are adequately trained to "deliver consistent and integrated advice on IT and business best practice".[190] Each of the four sponsors of the Initiative provided £250,000 funding during 1998/99 and a national launch is planned for January 2000.[191] The Government also told us that information technology skills in businesses would be a key priority of the University for Industry, when it is launched in autumn 2000.[192] During our briefing from British Telecommunications we were impressed by the productivity and competitiveness gains which could result from training small businessmen how to make best use of information and communications technologies, as demonstrated by the work of Professor Tony Davies in south Wales.[193] **We have reported previously on the uneven quality of advice available to SMEs;[194] it is to be hoped that the Advisor Skills Initiative and the University for Industry both contribute to an improvement, at least in relation to advice about information technology.**

74. There is a danger that, by focusing on the skills required by schoolchildren and entrepreneurs, that the bulk of the population, particularly those who do not work with personal computers or who are unable to afford them, might be overlooked.[195] Some initiatives to promote computer skills more widely in society have been launched. The Chancellor of the Exchequer announced in his 1999 Budget speech a tax exemption to encourage businesses to loan computer

---

[184] For instance, see www.earthlink.com
[185] See paragraph 80
[186] *Ev, p200 paragraph 5.2*
[187] HC Deb, 16 Mar 99, c606w; and see Employment and Education Committee, Third Report, Session 1998/99, *Highly Able Children*, HC22–I, paragraph 160
[188] *Survey of Information and Communications Technology in Schools 1998*, DfEE, Nov 98, on the internet at www.dfee.gov.uk/ict/results.htm
[189] *Ev, p4 section 8*; also *Ev, p28 paragraph 20*; and see paragraphs 83, 85 and 87–90
[190] *CWP*, paragraph 2.84; also see *Q117*; *Ev, p46 section 2.9*
[191] *Ev, p1 question 3a*; *CWP Implementation Plan*, section D3
[192] *Ev, p5 question 12*; *Q42*; *Ev, p200 paragraph 5.2*; and see *Financial Times*, 20 Apr 99, p12 and *Guardian*, 22 Jun 99, Higher Education section, p1
[193] *Ev, p13 annex 6*; also *Qq41, 111*; *Ev, p46 section 3.2*
[194] Trade and Industry Committee, Sixth Report, Session 1997/98, *Small and Medium Sized Enterprises*, HC774, paragraphs 8–12
[195] See *Q199*

equipment to their employees, drawing on the success of a similar Swedish scheme.[196] The Government's written memorandum contained reference to the "IT for All" programme, which it plans to extend to the most socially disadvantaged.[197] We are not convinced, however, that the "IT for All" programme has been high on any Ministerial list of priorities recently. A search for "IT for All" on the Government website currently yields no results, the "What's New" section of the "IT for All" website was until recently empty and the website itself has been frequently disabled.[198]

75. **Personal computers, the internet and electronic commerce should not be seen as exclusively playthings of the middle classes. We want to see everyone in society — rich or poor, young or old — able to take part in and benefit from electronic commerce. It will be a measure of the Government's success if, in five years time, the profile of the average internet user more closely resembles the population as a whole rather than being skewed towards young, university-educated men.[199] Aside from considerations of social justice and equity, widespread take-up of electronic commerce could provide immense benefits to British industry as well as cost savings for Government. We are of the impression that the Government shares our objective, but we think some more vocal advocacy and more dynamic policies, particularly in relation to socially disadvantaged groups, are called for. We recommend that Ministers, and the e-Envoy once appointed, give a lead in democratising and demystifying electronic commerce.**

### Employment

76. There has been speculation that the growth of electronic commerce will be detrimental to some sectors of the economy. Commercial intermediaries, such as travel agents and insurance brokers, might in future be by-passed by consumers seeking better deals on-line directly from service providers, such as airlines and underwriters.[200] We met with several major manufacturers in the US that are now selling their goods on their own internet sites as well as through their traditional distribution networks, which might suffer as a result. We have already mentioned the possibility of US internet sites becoming the equivalent of the High Street for British consumers in future.[201] The Government warned us of the "real risk that we will see UK markets, jobs and prosperity eroded by e-commerce competition from overseas" if UK firms do not seize the opportunities offered by electronic commerce.[202] Despite these predictions and suppositions, we are not aware of any analysis of how the growth of electronic commerce might affect employment in the UK or Europe. Discussions in the US confirmed the lack of research into this issue. Automation and computerisation have had a profound effect on the structure of the UK's industrial base over the last twenty years. The previous Secretary of State was adamant that "the economic landscape is changing — rapidly" and that "the knowledge-driven economy is the future."[203] **One of the burgeoning number of units within DTI might be well placed to research the implications for UK employment of the growth of electronic commerce, and we recommend that such research is carried out.**

### Universal Service

77. Several witnesses argued that universal service obligations should be established in relation to new information and communications technologies as they had been to basic telephony.[204] There are two elements to the concept of universal service obligations, as traditionally applied to the utility sectors. These are that:
   — certain services — such as a supply of electricity — are available to all consumers, on

---

[196] Inland Revenue Budget Press Notice IR6, 9 Mar 99

[197] Also see *Information and Communications Technology for the Elderly and People with Disabilities*, DTI, Oct 98, especially paragraph 5.11, on the internet at www.dti.gov.uk/cii/c23/index.html and see *Ev, p327 paragraph 3.6*

[198] www.itforall.org.uk; and see HC Deb, 19 Oct 98, c1045w

[199] *Ev, p86 paragraphs 2.3 and 8.1*; Fletcher Research published a survey of UK internet users in June 1999 which showed that 60% were male and 45% had a degree. The average age of internet users was 36 and the average household disposable income was £36,000 per annum — press release 29 Jun 99

[200] *Q57*

[201] See paragraph 8

[202] *Ev, p194 paragraph 2.5*

[203] DTI press releases 98/942, 25 Nov 98 and 98/953, 27 Nov 98

[204] *Q247; Ev, p89 paragraph 7.4, p263 section 2*

demand. It is illegal for suppliers to discriminate against consumers in the supply of such services on grounds such as the difficulty of supplying the service, or the income level of the consumer. Arrangements are required to be put in place to deal with consumers who have problems paying for the service

— the obligations to supply such services are placed on a defined group of businesses. Historically, these businesses have tended to be publicly-owned monopoly suppliers.

78. These two factors do not apply to any universal service obligations which might be considered in relation to electronic commerce. First, it would be difficult to define which services should be the subject of such obligations. The Government could mandate that all consumers be offered, or required, to be connected up to ISDN or DSL networks, for instance, but this would not be a technology-neutral approach and might have severe implications for UK competitiveness if alternative technologies, such as interactive TV or on-line access by mobile or satellite telephone systems, became predominant, and would also be prohibited by current EU law.[205] Unlike with electricity, gas or telephone connections in the past, firms and individuals are likely to participate in electronic commerce by numerous methods and means of connection in future. Nor is the market environment in relation to these technologies conducive to the introduction of universal service obligations. A multitude of competing operators, rather than a handful of monopoly suppliers, are seeking to offer on-line services.

79. **The conventional concept of universal service obligations does not apply to electronic commerce services.** The concept remains important, however. As we have argued, it is essential that everyone in society is able to share in the potential benefits of electronic commerce. We fully endorse the Government's view that a new division in society between those with access to knowledge, and the ability to make use of it, and those without such access or ability must not be allowed to develop. **There is an urgent need to find ways in which the universal service concept can be applied to electronic commerce.**

80. The Government has sought to achieve universal service goals in electronic commerce by improving access to information and communications technologies in several ways, including:[206]

— by setting up 800 IT Community Learning Centres in England
— a scheme for personal computers to be loaned to low income families
— a scheme for subsidised loans for the purchase of personal computers for home use by school teachers
— making available computers in public places such as libraries[207]
— negotiating reduced telephone tariff packages for internet access from schools (the National Grid for Learning) and, more recently, from other public institutions, such as libraries, Citizens Advice Bureaux and further education colleges.[208]

We have not examined the all important implementation of these schemes, but they illustrate the welcome commitment made by Government to consider how the universal service concept can be adapted to cover electronic commerce. This issue is also being considered at EU level during 1999 as part of the review of universal service in telecommunications.[209] **We recommend that the Government begin a national debate about how the universal service concept can be applied to electronic commerce.**

## IV BUSINESS SUPPORT

81. The Government announced a new target in the December 1998 Competitiveness White Paper, to triple the number of UK small and medium sized enterprises "wired up to the digital

---

[205] The EU Revised Voice Telephony and Interconnection Directives — *Regulating Communications: the way ahead*, DTI and DCMS, Jun 99, URN99/898, paragraph 3.73

[206] Ev, p2 question 7; and see DTI press notice 99/441, 25 May 99, on the information and communications technology "awareness day" held in Scotswood, Newcastle

[207] For more information on the provision of public access internet kiosks by Government see *Q194; Ev, p50 section 8.4, p289*

[208] HC Deb, 17 Jun 99, c554; OFTEL press notice 38/99, 5 Jul 99; *Q118* and DTI press notice 97/409, 18 Jun 97 on the National Grid for Learning. The National Grid for Learning website is at www.ngfl.gov.uk

[209] *Qq417–21*

market-place", from 350,000 at the beginning of 1998 to 1 million by 2002.[210] As we have seen, the most recent study of UK firms' use of external communications technologies has revealed that, already, around 600,000 firms are regular uses of such technologies.[211] In response, DTI has set three new, more challenging targets to be achieved by 2002:[212]

— 1.5 million small and medium sized enterprises to be regular users of external communications technologies
— 1 million small and medium sized enterprises to be "actually trading (ie purchasing or selling) on line"
— the performance of smaller firms in relation to information and communication technologies to be "up to the level of the best in the G7".

82. **The new targets set by Government are challenging**. We commented earlier on the limited use made of new information and communications technologies by companies with fewer than nine employees.[213] **There will need to be a step change in the attitude of very small firms to external communications technologies in order for the UK to catch up with the best of the G7 in this area.** Also, firms employing only 9% of the UK workforce currently sell goods on-line and firms employing 24% of the workforce make purchases on-line.[214] **Although it is not easy to tell how many firms are currently buying and selling on-line,[215] the target of having 1 million small and medium sized enterprises buying and selling on-line by 2002 will be significantly more difficult to achieve than that of having 1 million such firms regularly using information and communications technology by that date.**

### Competitiveness White Paper

83. DTI's strategy for achieving these targets was set out in the Competitiveness White Paper. We were told that "a wide range of initiatives are being taken forward with the Government's business partners in the Information Society Initiative", including:[216]

— completion of the national network of Local Support Centres by Autumn 1999, accompanied by an enhanced promotional campaign
— the Advisor Skills Initiative, referred to earlier[217]
— a Local Partnership Fund to increase use of information and communications technologies
— sectoral/supply chain seminars to develop use of information and communications technologies
— development of an E-Commerce Resource Centre on the Internet, available through the Enterprise Zone[218]
— the launch on 11 February 1999 of a new national award (the ISI/Interforum E-Commerce Awards) to recognise excellence in electronic commerce.[219]

84. The Government has promised "some £20 million extra", invested through the Information Society Initiative, to help fund the initiatives outlined above. We asked for a breakdown of how this new money would be allocated between projects during the three year period covered by the Competitiveness White Paper but were told, in May 1999, that individual funding allocations had not yet been made.[220] We were also surprised to discover, at the same time, how lacking in detail were several of the initiatives announced by DTI back in December 1998. We were told that

---

[210] *Ev, p200 paragraph 5.3*
[211] Paragraph 15
[212] Ev, pp6–7
[213] Paragraph 15
[214] *Benchmarking*, exhibit 6.22, p131
[215] *Benchmarking* bases its research on an assumption that there are 26.6 million company employees in the UK (p182) and does not publish a breakdown by number of employees of how many firms there are in the UK. DTI's 1997 small and medium sized enterprise statistics do include such a breakdown, but state that there were only 21.073 million company employees in the UK (on the internet at www.dti.gov.uk/SME4/pn98-597.htm). Using the DTI's 1997 assessment of the number of company employees in the UK, and the average number per company, around 900,000 firms employ 24% of the workforce, perhaps equivalent to the number of firms currently buying on-line
[216] *Ev, pp200–1 paragraph 5.4*
[217] Paragraph 73
[218] See *Ev, p4 section 8*
[219] *Ev, p4 section 8, pp259–60*
[220] Ev, p1 question 3

work on both the Local Partnership Fund and the supply chain seminars was at an "early stage" and that "no specific financial commitments" had been made towards them. Similarly, proposals for the E-Commerce Resource Centre were "currently being considered with a view to providing an effective and good value for money alternative to developing the Centre from scratch". The Competitiveness White Paper Implementation Plan states that several of the schemes announced in December 1998 will not be launched until December 1999 or January 2000.[221]

85. Another cause for concern is the extent to which the initiatives announced in the Competitiveness White Paper are coordinated with each other and with existing business support structures. Local Support Centres are the centrepiece of the Government's current IT business support strategy and are "embedded in the existing SMEs support infrastructure...eg Business Links in England and Wales".[222] The Local Partnership Fund is intended to be developed with "emerging RDAs in England and the Scottish Office, Welsh Office and Northern Ireland Office and the new Small Business Service".[223] It is not clear how Local Support Centres will relate to the Local Partnership Fund, RDAs and the new Small Business Service, or what will be the role of the devolved assemblies in developing and implementing policy in this area, including in relation to the development of regional strategies to help achieve the Government's targets for the participation of small and medium sized enterprises in electronic commerce.[224]

86. The Minister told us that "we need a communications strategy" for the initiatives detailed in the Competitiveness White Paper "to make sure they are reaching the people they are meant to reach in the way they are meant to reach them, to open up the horizons for them". When we asked about the communications strategy we found that it was rather less ambitious than the Minister described. We were told that it was "an internal media strategy" aimed at exploiting "newsworthy events" to do with the electronic commerce commitments made in the Competitiveness White Paper.[225]**There is a danger that the projects outlined in the Competitiveness White Paper are not capable of making a significant contribution towards the achievement of the ambitious goals set out by the Government in relation to the participation of small and medium sized enterprises in electronic commerce. Too many of the initiatives seem ill-thought out and lacking in detail — promising on paper, but, so far, short of substance. There is a worrying lack of attention to the coordination of these projects with existing initiatives, the proposed Small Business Service, new regional organisations and the devolved Assemblies.** The Competitiveness White Paper Implementation Plan has proved a useful tool for keeping track of the projects announced by DTI in December 1998. **We recommend that DTI publish details of progress made in implementing those initiatives relating to electronic commerce launched in the Competitiveness White Paper, how those initiatives are to be coordinated with regional and national bodies including the proposed Small Business Service, and how they will be evaluated in further Implementation Plans.**

### Local Support Centres

87. DTI told us that one finding of the 1999 International Benchmarking study was that "business use of Government initiatives and support organisations for access to information about information and communications technologies is high across the whole of the UK and is the highest of the G7 countries." Furthermore, "of those who use them, well over a third made successful changes to their businesses as a result, and over half felt that staff were knowledgeable and the advice relevant to their business." DTI concluded that "this demonstrates the importance that businesses in the UK place on the services supplied by the Government through Business Links and other organisations".[226] Local Support Centres are that part of the Business Links network specifically concerned with providing services relating to information

---

[221] *CWP Implementation Plan*, section D3: the E-Commerce Resource Centre is due to be launched in December 1999; the Adviser Skills Initiative and Local Partnership Fund are due to be launched in January 2000. "Initial research...to formulate proposals" to build on the sectoral/supply chain seminars is due to begin in December 1999

[222] Ev, pp1–2 question 4

[223] Ev, p1 questions 3b–d

[224] *Ev, p201 paragraph 5.5*; also *Q590*

[225] Ev, p2 question 6; *Q581*

[226] Ev, pp6–7

and communications technologies. We have long taken an interest in the Business Link network, including Local Support Centres, focusing on whether they fully meet the needs of business and provide the taxpayer with value for money.[227]

88. We asked DTI how it had evaluated Local Support Centres to date and were told that 60,000 firms had used the Centres in the last twelve months. Evaluation of their usefulness involved:[228]

— each Centre providing monitoring reports to Government every six months. "Customer satisfaction rates reported are 85% plus"
— existing monitoring of Business Links, which is soon to be supplemented by the publication of information about the impact Business Link services, including Local Support Centres, have on the profitability, turnover, productivity and export performance of assisted companies
— identification of best practice for Local Support Centres to follow and of areas of weak performance to be addressed
— an "internal economic evaluation" of the Information Society Initiative, which is about to commence.

89. We asked the Federation of Small Businesses for its views on Local Support Centres. In oral evidence they said that "Business Links have very little IT knowledge...and if we get down to e-commerce there is very little knowledge of it unfortunately...Business Links are not providing the service...to the people they are supposed to be assisting".[229] Rather than use Business Links services for advice on information and communications technology, the Federation told us that "the average age of an [IT] consultant in small business was 14 — it was the sons and daughters".[230] **Small businesses remain unpersuaded of the usefulness of Business Link services, including Local Support Centres, as providers of advice on electronic commerce.**

90. In reply to a parliamentary written question, DTI recently published details of the "local electronic commerce support centres" available in the north west of England. These included twelve "Information Society Initiative centres"; seven (soon to be eight) Technology Management Centres operated by North West Technology Web; the Connect centre in Liverpool; and the ISaware and Gemisis centres in Greater Manchester.[231] The different organisations each recorded usage of their centres in different ways. 2,523 firms had used the twelve Information Society Initiative centres between April and December 1998 while only 350 firms were recorded as using the Gemisis centre between mid-1996 and the end of 1998.[232] e centre[UK] told us that Local Support Centres and related organisations "need stronger focus and drive from the centre".[233] **We are not convinced that it is desirable for the Government to sponsor the provision of advice on information and communications technology to firms through a hotch-potch of seemingly unrelated organisations. A greater degree of national consistency is required. We recommend that steps are taken to improve the consistency and coordination of the electronic commerce support services offered to small and medium sized enterprises, including clarification of the relationship between Local Support Centres and the proposed Small Business Service.**

---

[227] Trade and Industry Committee, Fifth Report, 1996/97, *Business Links*, HC302; Sixth Report, 1997/98, *Small and Medium Sized Enterprises*, HC774, especially paragraphs 8–13; we heard evidence from Michael Wills MP, Under-Secretary of State, DTI, on small and medium sized enterprises on 17 March; the budget allocated to Local Support Centres by DTI for the 1997–2000 period can be found in HC Deb, 19 Apr 99, c453w
[228] Ev, pp2–3 question 4
[229] *Q86*
[230] *Q92*
[231] HC Deb, 1 Feb 99, c513w
[232] Letter from Michael Wills MP to Lindsay Hoyle MP, 26 April 1998 (see HC Deb, 1 Feb 99, c513w)
[233] *Ev, p4 section 8*

**On-Line Business Support**

91. Websites have become an important aspect of the Government's business support strategy. Each Government department and agency has its own website, facilitating access to press notices, consultation documents, command papers, ministerial speeches and the like. DTI has also been involved with the establishment of the Information Society and Enterprise Zone websites, which are aimed at encouraging small and medium sized enterprises to get on-line and to provide them with a starting point to exploring the internet.[234] The Federation of Small Businesses told us about its similarly focused initiative.[235] DTI has also recently launched several internet resources aimed at specific business needs, particularly those of exporters.[236] **We welcome the increasing use made of the internet to provide business support services. DTI should ensure that its on-line services are coordinated with the business support services it sponsors off-line.**

92. The Federation of Small Businesses told us that many small and medium sized enterprises would find it useful for the Government to expand the amount of information it made available for free on-line. In particular, the Federation argued that the entire statute book should be available on-line, to assist firms' awareness of and compliance with legislation.[237] At present, almost all Acts of Parliament since 1996 and statutory instruments since 1997 are available on–line.[238] Older legislation, including references to such legislation in more recent statutes, is not available on-line. **Particularly given the frequency with which new laws refers back to older pieces of legislation, we recommend that the Government consider placing all primary and secondary legislation currently in force on-line.**

## V ELECTRONIC GOVERNMENT

93. Central to the Government's electronic commerce agenda are the commitments made in relation to its own use of the electronic environment. These include that:[239]
—    90% by volume of all routine procurement of goods by central government are to be done electronically by March 2001[240]
—    25% by volume of all Government services are to be available electronically by 2002; 50% by 2005 and 100% by 2008.

The Central Information Technology Unit (CITU) has recently published a useful assessment of the progress made to date in relation to these targets, broken down by department.[241] Further assessments are due to appear on a six-monthly basis. DTI gave us an assessment of how the department expected to meet the targets set both in relation to procurement and making its services available electronically.[242]

94. DTI lies close to the heart of the electronic Government agenda. Proposals regarding the legal status of electronic signatures, and the promotion of digital signatures, on which we reported recently, underpin many of the services which the Government hopes to introduce in electronic format.[243] DTI has been involved in a number of high-profile electronic Government initiatives, including the introduction of electronic export licence application forms and the Post Office's controversial Horizon project, both of which we have recently inquired into.[244] The Government explained in detail its plans to allow firms to file VAT and PAYE returns electronically.[245] DTI has also established a number of internet resources, including many to help

---

[234] The Enterprise Zone is at www.enterprisezone.org.uk; the Information Society Initiative website's address is www.isi.gov.uk; *Q88*

[235] *Qq77–80*; also DTI press notice 98/970, 1 Dec 98

[236] DTI press notices 99/312, 12 Apr 99; 99/376, 5 May 99; 99/524, 18 Jun 99; and 99/573, 30 Jun 99; 99/576, 6 Jul 99

[237] *Qq 94–5*

[238] The internet address is www.hmso.gov.uk/legis.htm; Local Acts passed before 1997 are not on-line; for plans for the launch of a Statute Law Database, which may or may not be accessible on–line; see HL Deb, 16 Dec 98, cwa 157

[239] *Ev, pp200-1, paragraph 4.49*

[240] On Government procurement see *Q69*; *Ev, p3 sections 6–7*; *pp11–13, annex 5, p51 section 10.3, p223 paragraph 48, p266 paragraph 16, p275 paragraph 4.7*; and HC Deb, 19 Oct 98, cc1051–2w

[241] *Progress Report: Electronic Government 25% Target*, Cabinet Office, May 99 (hereafter *CITU Report*)

[242] Ev, pp2–4 question 8

[243] *Ev, p200 paragraph 4.50*

[244] Ev, pp20–1 *Qq438–44*; and on the DTI's own computerisation programme see DTI press notice 98/920, 20 Nov 98

[245] Ev, p4 question 9

small and medium sized enterprises, for instance in relation to export opportunities.[246] CITU's analysis shows that DTI and its executive agencies have approximately 9.2 million dealings with the public per year, including payments, of which 23% can be conducted electronically. It is anticipated that 84% of these dealings will be capable of being conducted electronically by 2002.[247]

95. CITU's recent analysis of progress made to date in making Government services available on-line and our inquiries into DTI's part in that progress lead us to draw a number of general conclusions about the electronic Government agenda:

— **CITU's analysis shows that most Departments already provide more than 25% of their services by volume electronically. The 2002 target is therefore not particularly challenging, although the 2008 target might prove a challenge to some departments.**[248] It is worth remembering that there is a major difference between a service being available electronically (eg on a floppy disk) and being available on-line, however

— **Making a service available electronically is no guarantee that anyone will wish to use it in that way.** The Open for Business pilot project in Norwich, in which the Post Office provided a one-stop-shop for businesses to interact with Government, was used by only a tiny number of firms.[249] Although the Post Office told us that "the very few people who actually used it found it extremely beneficial" and that, for them, it was a "very valuable learning experience" **it is essential that the electronic Government agenda is driven by the needs and requirements of users, not by what Government officials assume these to be**

— Several high-profile electronic Government projects have not progressed smoothly. The computerisation of the national insurance system has been the subject of critical reports by the National Audit Office and the Public Accounts Committee;[250] the computerisation of the Passports Agency has caused problems in recent months;[251] and we will report soon on the considerable difficulties associated with the Post Office's Horizon project. Such projects have been "complex and adventurous", seeking to bring "a lot of government departments [and] a lot of software and technology suppliers" together, often under the auspices of a private finance initiative, and have sometimes failed to meet their ambitious timescales or to live up to their grandiose aims[252]

— Many witnesses argued that the Government has an important role to play in encouraging electronic commerce by successfully implementing its own projects.[253] **High-profile failures to implement electronic Government projects send out the wrong signals to the private sector about the potential attractions and benefits of electronic commerce.**

96. **We are concerned that the electronic Government agenda is characterised by hyperbole, over-optimism about the capabilities of management to implement novel technological systems on a large scale, and repeated failures to learn from past mistakes. There is an urgent need for a hard-headed assessment, across Government, of what electronic services are required by users and how these best can be delivered and financed. However desirable and convenient they may be in theory, ambitious cross-departmental**

---

[246] For instance see DTI press notices 99/312, 12 Apr 99; 99/376, 5 May 99; 99/524, 18 Jun 99; 99/573, 30 Jun 99; 99/576, 6 Jul 99

[247] *CITU Report*, pp24–6; at present Companies House is responsible for 7.5 million of the transactions recorded as being the responsibility of DTI and that agency's computerisation programme is primarily responsible for DTI being on course to easily meet the 2002 target

[248] *Ev, p275 paragraph 4.3*

[249] Ev, pp20–1; *Qq445–6*; *Government Computing*, Jun 99, p6 reported that only 11 firms had registered with the pilot project

[250] *The Contract to Develop and Operate the Replacement National Insurance Recording System*, National Audit Office, 1997/98, HC12; Public Accounts Committee, Forty-sixth Report, 1997/98, *The Contract to Develop and Update the Replacement National Insurance Recording System*, HC472; Treasury Minute on the Forty-second, Forty-sixth, Forty-seventh and Fifty-seventh Reports from the Committee of Public Accounts, 1997/98, Sep 98, Cm4041; Public Accounts Committee, Twenty-second Report, 1998/99, *Delays to the National Insurance Recording System*, HC182

[251] For instance see HC Deb, 29 Jun 99, cc140–96

[252] The quotations are taking from *Q445*; and see *Ev, pp223–4 paragraphs 47, 49–55*

[253] *Qq43, 68, 194, 219*; *Ev, p28 paragraph 18, p52 section 10.6, p111 section 10*

**projects and "one-stop-shops" are of no use to man nor beast unless they can be delivered on time, in budget, and in full working order. The current plague of costly, late and untested electronic Government projects must be tackled before the situation worsens.**

97. We would also wish to draw attention to the concerns raised, in quite different contexts, by Age Concern and by a group of Christians opposed to the use of computer technology.[254] **Care must be taken to ensure that those who cannot use new technologies, or those who, for whatever reasons, choose not to do so, are not discriminated against because of the rush to embrace electronic commerce.**

### Privacy

98. The Data Protection Registrar warned us of the potential tensions between proposals for the establishment of "single points of contact" between firms and individuals and Government services and data protection legislation. She suggested that "there is a temptation to use data collected for one purpose for something completely different and it is not difficult to see that the citizen may be reluctant to make use of the one stop shop if he mistrusts the ways in which any information which he provides may be used".[255] She cited, as an example, the Social Security Administration (Fraud) Act 1997 which permits the disclosure of information by the Inland Revenue and Customs and Excise to the Department of Social Security (DSS), the exchange of information between the DSS and local authorities, and the exchange of information between different local authorities. The Registrar told us that, during the passage of the Bill, she had called for a statutory Code of Practice setting out the standards by which the public bodies specified in the Act must operate and the rights of individuals to redress, where appropriate. The Government conceded a voluntary Code of Practice covering only the activities of the DSS, which, the Registrar commented, was now reflected in the number of complaints she was receiving about alleged misuse of data by local authorities.[256] **The Government has a duty to set the highest standards of data protection in its own electronic commerce projects.**

### DTI's Websites

99. We discussed earlier the use made by DTI of websites to provide information and support to small and medium sized enterprises.[257] DTI maintains or contributes to a number of other websites, aside from those concerned with business support, including for the Foresight programme, the Low Pay Commission and in relation to the provision of technical telecommunications information. We asked DTI in1998 how it measured the usage of the websites it maintained; how it advertised its websites; and how the content of its websites were monitored.[258] DTI told us that it had set up an Internet Editorial Board to "oversee all aspects of internet publishing" and that it had appointed an internet publicity manager in 1996 to manage the content of the main departmental website on a day to day basis. The Internet Editorial Board has commissioned a review of the department's website which is intended to ensure that DTI can meet its target of 25% of transactions with the public being capable of electronic delivery by 2002. **DTI should seek to ensure that its websites remain up-to-date, well organised and operative in order so that they become an increasingly important means of disseminating information and facilitating contact with the public.**

## VI NEW CHALLENGES

100. As well as generating new policy debates — on encryption, for instance — electronic commerce introduces new dimensions to many existing debates, including in relation to taxation, intellectual property rights and consumer protection. The issues raised by electronic commerce in each of these cases are not entirely original, but the speed with which transactions can be completed electronically, the scope for individual consumers to engage in such transactions, the potential anonymity of such transactions and the ease with which cross-border trade can be

---

[254] *Ev, pp227, 326–7 and Qq249–50; Ev, p89 paragraph 7.7*

[255] *Ev, p175 paragraph 30 and see Ev, p224 paragraphs 56–9*; see also Fifteenth Annual Report of the Data Protection Registrar, Jun 99, HC 595, pp 20–5 and Appendix 4

[256] *Ev, pp307–8 section 2*

[257] Paragraph 91

[258] Trade and Industry Committee, Minutes of Evidence, 4 Nov 98, *The Work of the Department of Trade and Industry, 1997/98*, HC1138, pp5–6 section 5; and see HC Deb, 16 Feb 98, c664w

conducted on-line all serve to call into question the adequacy of existing arrangements. One consideration, above all others, is common to all of the issues discussed below. Electronic commerce is inherently global, implying that individual countries cannot legislate for their own taxation, intellectual property and other regimes independently of the rest of the world. As an example of this trend, Mr Reed of the Centre for Commercial Law Studies, Queen Mary and Westfield College, cited the UK's restrictions on the advertising of financial services which were now daily infringed by the websites of financial services firms established overseas.[259]Global discussions relating to electronic commerce have begun in a variety of fora to reflect the need for worldwide solutions; the results of failure to achieve international agreements, for instance in relation to data protection, have already manifested themselves. **Electronic commerce is eroding national, and regional, boundaries in many different policy areas.**

## Taxation

101. The Government has set out four broad principles which it believes should be applied to the taxation of electronic commerce, namely that taxation should be:[260]

— *technology-neutral*, so that the means by which a transaction is conducted does not influence the way in which it is taxed
— *certain and transparent*
— *effective*, so that double-taxation and unintended taxation are avoided and the risks of evasion minimised
— *efficient*, in order that compliance costs are minimised.

Other Governments, most notably the US Administration, have evinced similar principles.[261]

102. In its written memorandum to us, the Government said that "there is no need for major changes to existing rules, or for the introduction of new taxes" to deal with electronic commerce in the short run but that changes to national and international tax rules might be needed thereafter.[262] The Chartered Institute of Taxation echoed these remarks, stating that "the present UK tax system will cope satisfactorily with electronic commerce...we do not think any new powers are required".[263] Witnesses from the business world tended to support the Government's principles and oppose new taxes on electronic commerce.[264] Inland Revenue and HM Customs and Excise have issued a joint paper outlining the potential tax implications of electronic commerce.[265] These include:

— the treatment of services, including software, music and other "goods" capable of being downloaded from the internet, for VAT purposes, when sold to consumers over the internet[266]
— whether payments made to download and make use of copyrighted material from the internet should be taxed as royalties, and how such taxation can be collected
— the relevance of the concept of the place of permanent establishment for non-residents in relation to electronic commerce.[267]

103. We received some helpful memoranda on the practical problems posed to the tax authorities by electronic commerce,[268] including a useful exchange of correspondence between Derek Wyatt MP and Dawn Primarolo MP, Financial Secretary, HM Treasury.[269] Ms Primarolo's

---

[259] *Q263; Ev, p99 section 4*; and *Ev, p244 section 2*
[260] *Net Benefit*, DTI, Oct 98, URN 98/895, p17; and *Ev, p197 paragraph 4.19*; we deal with the issue of customs duty in paragraphs 127–9
[261] *Ev, p53 annex 1 paragraph A1.2* and *Independent*, 27 Feb 98, p11 but see *Ev, p221 paragraph 30* on US plans for a digital stamp tax
[262] *Ev, p197 paragraph 4.21*
[263] *Ev, p270*
[264] *Ev, p27 paragraph 13, p110 section 8, p282, p304 question 1*
[265] *Electronic Commerce: UK Tax Policy*, Inland Revenue and HM Customs and Excise, 6 Oct 98; an overview of the issues has also been provided by C. Anne Fairpo, *The Tax Journal*, 9 Nov 98
[266] There is an emerging consensus that, as far as their tax treatment is concerned, "goods" delivered over the internet should be regarded as services; see paragraph 126 for the debate concerning how such "goods" such be classified for trade purposes
[267] See *Ev, p268, p275 paragraph 3.10, p282*
[268] For instance from the Chartered Institute of Taxation, *Ev, pp267–70* and the British Bankers' Association *pp274–5, section 3*
[269] *Ev, pp299–300*

letter makes a number of important points:

— although the taxation of goods ordered over the internet but delivered by traditional physical means might be complicated, such goods cannot normally escape taxation levied on goods bought off-line and, in the case of goods ordered over the internet from abroad, would often also be liable for customs duty

— tax due on "goods" which are downloaded from the internet can be difficult to collect. In the case of such "goods" provided by firms outside of the EU and downloaded by persons not registered for VAT purposes, there is currently no practical means of collecting the tax due

— Although "the internet makes it easier for residents of the UK to buy goods and services from overseas companies which do not have a presence in the UK sufficient to require them to pay corporation tax" UK firms might have increased opportunities to sell overseas and, thus, "there could be an overall increase in our tax revenues" resulting from increased electronic commerce.

104. The complications to national taxation rules resulting from electronic commerce might encourage some firms to exploit potential loopholes — for instance, by registering the permanent establishment of their websites or internet businesses in low-tax environments, such as the Channel Islands, or by attempting to avoid such registration altogether. Mr Wyatt's letter raised this possibility, by citing the example of a car ordered from a firm registered in the Cayman Islands.[270] Witnesses were generally sanguine about the possibility of the internet assisting wide-scale tax avoidance, although concerns have been expressed in relation to betting and gaming duties.[271] Mr Reed, of the Centre for Commercial Law Studies, Queen Mary and Westfield College, told us that "there is now a bookmaker operating out of Alderney offering UK citizens the opportunity to bet on horse races free of betting tax".[272] The Betting Office Licensees' Association sent us a memorandum outlining some of their concerns with regard to internet gambling.[273] **We welcome the Government's indication that it will play an active role in the international efforts to safeguard national taxation revenues from a proliferation of low-tax or tax-free internet gambling facilities.**

105. Mr Agar, Deputy Director General of the Confederation of British Industry told us that he was "fairly confident" that international agreement, at least between the US and EU, could be reached on a framework for dealing with tax issues.[274] The OECD is the main forum for negotiations on international tax issues and much work was done prior to the October 1998 Ottawa conference, when a two-year programme of future work was agreed.[275] Witnesses have identified the taxation of international sales of "goods" delivered over the internet to private consumers as the major impediment to agreement being reached.[276] Mr Reed described this issue as "a nightmare", from which he could not see an escape at present.[277] Problems with the levying of sales taxes on electronic transactions are particularly acute in federal countries, including the US, where differing local tax regimes may operate. The EU has begun consulting with businesses about the VAT treatment of electronic commerce.[278] APACS told us that one proposal was for VAT to be collected by credit card companies as payment transactions are processed, but this raised practical concerns, as well as questions of security and privacy which we discussed with the Data Protection Registrar.[279]

---

[270] *Ev, p299*

[271] *Q58; Ev, pp269–70*; but see *Q217*

[272] *Q254; Ev, p197 paragraph 4.27*; and see *The Express*, 28 May 99 and *Financial Times*, 21 Jun 99, p5

[273] *The Potential Impact of Off-Shore Betting on Government Tax Revenues*, 17 Jun 99; and see paragraph 8 for an estimate of the revenues generated by internet gambling

[274] *Q73*

[275] *Ev, p197 paragraphs 4.22–4.23*; key OECD documents from the Ottawa conference include *Electronic Commerce: Taxation Framework Conditions* and *Electronic Commerce: a discussion paper on taxation issues*, Committee on Fiscal Affairs; the impact of electronic commerce on VAT is being considered at EU level

[276] Eg *Q73; Ev, p45 section 7.3, p304 question 1* and see footnotes 278 and 279 on VAT

[277] *Q271*

[278] *Ev, p37 paragraphs 8–9, p110 section 8, pp268–9, p274 paragraphs 3.3–3.9, p282*; DGXXI of the European Commission issued a "non-paper" on "Thoughts about possible modification to the 6th VAT Directive" on 4 Jan 99; on VAT issues see "Electronic Challenge", P. Jenkins, *Taxation*, 29 Oct 98 and "Electronic Commerce: the VAT barriers, J. Kennedy, *Tolley's Practical VAT Service*, Vol. 12, No. 9, Sep 98

[279] *Qq297–306, 490–1; Ev, pp115 annex D, pp121, 282*

106. **The world's major economies broadly agree on the principles which should underpin the taxation of electronic commerce.** The US Internet Tax Freedom Act 1998, for instance, prevents new taxes on electronic commerce, such as a "bit" tax on the volume of information flowing over the internet, from being introduced for three years and established a federal commission to examine local and federal tax policies in the US.[280] We discussed the future work of the Commission during our recent visit to the US.[281] **Rapid progress in reaching agreement on how the international tax system should be adjusted to take account of electronic commerce is unlikely, however. The issues are not only complicated but, especially in relation to sales taxes, solutions are hoped for rather than expected to be found. There is also a danger that the broad principles which it is agreed should underpin the taxation of electronic commerce might be undermined by compromises and agreements reached on issues which, although minor in themselves, have unintended and unwelcome cumulative effects. The slow pace of policy development might prove advantageous, in that it could ensure any agreement reached is not overtaken by technological developments or unforeseen consumer trends. We would welcome frequent updates from the UK tax authorities on progress made on reaching international agreements in this area.**

### Intellectual Property Rights

107. The CBI told us that "digital technologies and e-commerce, by their nature, threaten effective intellectual property rights (IPR)" and many witnesses stressed the need for the existing IPR regime to be adapted to cope with the on-line environment.[282] Intellectual property rights are essential components of an economy in which knowledge and information are used to generate wealth.[283] Copyright is the intellectual property right potentially most at risk from the development of digital and on-line technologies, because of the "ease with which material can be disseminated via the new networks (and used or copied)".[284] The Government told us that it would also be assessing the practical consequences of electronic commerce for other intellectual property rights, including patents and designs.[285]

108. The Computing Services and Software Association reminded us that digitisation, rather than the growth of electronic commerce, had made piracy and other IPR infringements much easier to accomplish.[286] It argued that, although the internet could be used to distribute pirate copies of software and music, electronic commerce could also have the opposite effect, for instance by making it easier to get hold of software from manufacturers.[287] The need for IPR protection to be updated to deal with the effects of digitisation has meant that, at the international level, much work has already been done. Two IPR treaties were agreed under the auspices of the World Intellectual Property Organisation in 1996 and further work there is continuing.[288] IPRs are also seen as a "strategic part of the comprehensive work programme on electronic commerce agreed at the second WTO ministerial council".[289]

109. The WIPO treaties have yet to be ratified by the UK, and will not be until the amended draft EU Directive on Copyright and Related Rights in the Information Society is agreed and transposed into national law, although the Government has indicated that the possibility of the amended draft Directive being implemented by 30 June 2000, as planned, is "an increasingly unrealistic goal".[290] The Government told us that "UK copyright law already provides a sound

---

[280] *Ev, p53 annex 1 paragraph 1.2*

[281] The Commission's website can be found at www.cns.state.va.us/e_commerce/index.htm

[282] *Ev, p27 paragraphs 11–12 and p110 section 7*

[283] We have recently reported on a range of issues related to IPRs, in our Eighth Report, 1998/99, *Trade Marks, Fakes and Consumers*, HC380

[284] *Ev, p197 paragraph 4.29 Ev, p197 paragraph 4.29*; and see *Independent*, 17 Jun 99 on a US court ruling that devices capable of recording music from the internet do not infringe laws which aim to prevent serial re-recording of copyrighted music

[285] *Ev, p198, paragraph 4.36, p291 question 3*

[286] *Q185*; and see *Financial Times*, 2 Feb 99, p8

[287] *Q187*; but see *Mirror*, 2 Jun 99, "Mirror Money" section, p8

[288] *Ev, p198 paragraphs 4.32–4.33*; on future work see *World Trade Agenda*, No. 99/1, 9 Mar 99 pp11–13

[289] *Ev, p198 paragraph 4.34*

[290] European Scrutiny Committee, Twenty–third Report, 1998/99, HC34–xxiii, pxiv paragraph 2.7; and see HC Deb, 13 Jul 99, c156w

basis to meet the challenges of new technology" but that it broadly welcomed the clarification and European harmonisation offered by the amended draft Directive.[291] The Post Office, however, described the draft Directive as "controversial, as it would change existing copyright law unnecessarily, and would not make any provision for future flexibility".[292] Several points of controversy have been raised during consideration of the proposed directive and we received a number of memoranda about these, particularly including the status of incidental copies of web pages stored temporarily by internet service providers which it was feared might be held to infringe copyright.[293]

110. Another issue often raised with us, both during our inquiry and in the US, concerned the extent to which internet service providers should be held liable for material posted on the websites and newsgroups they hosted.[294] This issue is touched upon by the amended draft Copyright directive and the draft Legal Aspects of Electronic Commerce directive.[295] Several recent court cases have complicated matters, particularly in relation to whether or not service providers can be held responsible for IPR infringements.[296] Service providers have argued that their role is akin to telephone companies, which are not held liable for the messages they carry, whereas rights holders have insisted that internet firms should be treated in the same way as conventional publishers.[297] This is an extremely serious issue where legal clarity is urgently required — one US internet firm told us that it would pull out of the European markets if the directives were unduly biased towards rights holders. **We welcome the Government's commitment to ensuring that a "fair balance is achieved between rights holders and users": once that has been achieved at European level it must be swiftly transposed into UK law in order to clarify the present legal position in several vital areas.**

111. The Competitiveness White Paper included an IPR Action Plan which made reference to several initiatives which the Government would pursue in relation to electronic commerce.[298] These included "stronger protection for software-related inventions". The UK recently hosted "a major international conference on ways to protect computer software" which is expected to lead to a draft EU directive on the harmonisation of EU patent laws as they relate to software.[299] The Post Office emphasised the importance of this issue, arguing that "the difficulty of obtaining a patent in the UK for computer software deters inventors from seeking protection they would gain as a matter of course in the United States, and this leaves UK businesses at a competitive disadvantage."[300]Another aspect of the IPR Action Plan was a proposal to "introduce a worldwide system for electronic trading in IPR". This system would enable the Patent Office to "accept electronic filings and payments relating to international applications, prepared according to internationally agreed standards, and to forward applications and payments electronically to WIPO and the European Patent Office".[301]

INTERNET DOMAIN NAMES

112. Computers locate each other by means of unique Internet Protocol numbers, which may be long and not particularly memorable.[302] In order to assist users, Internet Protocol codes are converted into domain names — for instance, www.parliament.uk. These can allow internet users to link easily website addresses to physical organisations and facilitate passage around the internet by the use of bookmarks and intelligent guesswork.

---

[291] *Ev, p198 paragraph 4.30*; and see *Trade Marks, Fakes and the Consumer*, Ev, p147 paragraphs 5.4–5.6

[292] *Ev, p154 section 4*

[293] for instance *Qq211–4; Ev, p35, p48 sections 6.4–6.7 , p63, p82 section 3; Daily Telegraph*, Connected section, p3, 18 Feb 99

[294] for instance *Qq211–2; Ev, p35, pp48–9 sections 6.8–6.10; p82 section 3, p291 question 3, p292 question 1*

[295] *Draft Directive on Copyright and Related Rights in the Information Society*, Dec 97, Com97(628); and *Draft Directive on Legal Aspects of Electronic Commerce*, Nov 98, Com(98)586

[296] For a case involving Demon Internet see *The Times*, 27 Mar 99, p26

[297] *Ev, p154 section 4*

[298] *CWP*, p56

[299] HC Deb, 29 Jun 99, c88w

[300] *Ev, p154 section 4*

[301] Trade and Industry Committee, Eighth Report, Session 1998/99, *Trade Marks, Fakes and Consumers*, Ev, p265, paragraphs 4.1–4.4

[302] *Ev, pp198–9 paragraphs 4.37–4.40* on internet domain names

113. The UK domain name system is run by a private firm — Nominet — with whom organisations must register to receive a UK website address (for instance, ending .uk). Until recently, the US system, which is responsible for the commercially attractive .com label amongst others, was operated by the US Government. This was a controversial arrangement, not least because of the complex, new trademark issues which have arisen in this area. There have recently been a number of cases involving organisations or individuals registering several internet domain names which have led to trademark infringement actions as well as genuine clashes between firms of the same name in different countries seeking to register the same domain name.[303]

114. The US Government issued a White Paper in June 1998 which set out proposals to transfer governance of the US internet domain system to a private firm. The European Union worked with the US Government to ensure that European interests were adequately represented in the new arrangement and, on 26 October 1998, the Board of Directors of the new body, the Internet Corporation for Assigned Names and Numbers, was appointed. **We welcome the swift progress made in resolving tensions between the EU and US concerning the allocation of domain names.**

**Consumer Protection**

115. Consumers must consider a number of issues when they purchase goods, particularly when transactions are not made face-to-face with the retailer.[304] In particular, consumers need to be confident that:

— the goods they purchase match those described to them by the retailer
— the retailer takes no more money from them than was agreed
— any financial information imparted is secure from interception or from being passed on to third parties
— the goods are safe and sound; and that if they are not they can be easily repaired or replaced
— if ordered and paid for in advance, the goods will be delivered
— if a dispute arises, the legal jurisdiction under which the transaction took place is clear and that access to redress is relatively easy.

116. **In many respects, transactions which make use of a computer are no different from mail-order or telephone transactions.** Existing consumer protection legislation has proved flexible in the face of challenges arising from such transactions, and new legislation has been introduced where thought necessary.[305] Electronic commerce transactions do pose some new challenges to existing consumer protection regimes, however, including:[306]

— the increased possibility of fraud, for instance because of the ease with which internet sites can be established anonymously to sell fictional goods by order and then removed once it becomes obvious that the goods "sold" are not being delivered
— the absence of a physical "real world" presence for some internet retail ventures, which can cause difficulties for consumers with complaints or requiring refunds or after-sales service
— the difficulty of defining where a website is established for legal purposes and the ease with which cross-border transactions can take place, both of which can cause problems for consumers when disputes arise.

There are essentially two issues for the Government to address in relation to on-line consumer protection. First, how to protect the unwary from scams and rogue traders operating on the internet and, secondly, how to ensure that consumers can conduct transactions electronically in a clear and consistent legal environment, in which redress when things go wrong is as easy to obtain as it would be off-line.

---

[303] For instance see *Financial Times*, 10 Mar 99, p38 and 4 May 99; "Domain Name Registration, Regulation and Assignment", C. Gordon-Pullar, *Communications Law*, Vol. 2, No. 4, 1997
[304] *Ev, p283 paragraph 4, p243*
[305] For instance, the Distance Selling Directive, see *Qq43, 230, 489; Ev, p48 section 5.3, p88 paragraph 5.1, p153 section 3, p233 paragraph*, HC Deb, 30 Mar 98, c384w, 14 Jan 99, c248w
[306] *Ev, p87 paragraph 3.2, pp243–4 section 1*

117. In relation to the first issue, the Office of Fair Trading (OFT) told us that "dubious offers and scams will usually be accessible by anyone anywhere. Preventing such harmful practices raises various complex legal issues". The main problem is that rogue traders are likely to exploit the anonymity offered by the internet to the full, making it difficult to establish for sure the identity of the firm or individual responsible for a sharp practice. This problem is compounded by the possibility that the victim of the sharp practice may reside in a different country or even a different continent to the rogue trader.[307] International collaboration between regulatory authorities is essential to search out the perpetrators of scams and sharp practices. The OFT told us of the establishment of the International Marketing Supervision Network, which had undertaken two Internet Sweep Days to warn websites showing "dubious 'get rich quick' schemes and 'miracle' health claims that they needed to comply with the law".[308] Commendable though such activity is, we suspect that it catches only a small fraction of dishonest internet sites.

118. The second issue is being addressed primarily at EU level. The draft Legal Aspects of Electronic Commerce Directive aims to define the legal jurisdiction which will apply to electronic commerce transactions; when an electronic commerce transaction takes place; the place of establishment of internet businesses; and how effective redress can be secured.[309] The draft Directive has been broadly welcomed by UK businesses and consumer groups.[310] One significant controversy has concerned the question of which law applies in cross-border electronic transactions — the law of the consumer's home country, or that of the vendor's. The draft Directive envisages the vendor's domestic law applying to such transactions — the 'country of origin' principle — something many business organisations favoured.[311] The Consumers in Europe Group told us that this was contrary to the provisions of the OECD draft guidelines for electronic commerce and of the EU Council of Ministers Resolution on the Consumer Dimension of the Information Society. It argued that application of the 'country of origin' principle would force consumers "to rely on unfamiliar practices, or to make choices based not on the goods or services they are buying, but on the legal systems they are about to buy into".[312] Mr Reed of the Centre for Commercial Law Studies, Queen Mary and Westfield College, thought that the 'country of origin' principle might not be enforceable in UK courts.[313] Fears have also been raised that firms might seek to establish internet operations in the EU states offering the least stringent consumer protection standards if the 'country of origin' principle were introduced, and that states might compete to drop their consumer protection standards in order to attract businesses.[314]

119. DTI pointed out, in their response to the consultation exercise on the draft Directive, that if the 'country of origin' principle did not apply to electronic commerce transactions then firms would need to be aware of the legal provisions relevant to each member state of the EU.[315] Instead, if the Directive is agreed, then the burden will lie on consumers to understand the relevant law in each member state. **Electronic commerce transactions, although often carried out in a consumer's home or work place, might have the same legal status as transactions made abroad, for instance when a consumer is on holiday, as a result of the implementation of the draft EU Legal Aspects of Electronic Commerce Directive. It is vital that, when buying on the internet, consumers are made fully aware of the jurisdiction under which the transaction is taking place. The development of a single EU electronic commerce market is likely to increase pressure for the harmonisation of consumer protection legislation. Such harmonisation must not involve any reduction in the level of protection currently offered to consumers by UK legislation.**

---

[307] *Ev, p283 paragraph 6* and see *p326 paragraph 2.2*

[308] *Ev, p284, paragraphs 9–10* and *Qq228, 232*

[309] For discussions of other issues see *Ev, p234 paragraphs 7–11, pp276–7 annex A, p281*

[310] Letter from Michael Wills MP, Under-Secretary of State, DTI, to Lord Tordoff, Chairman of the Select Committee on the European Communities, 29 April 1999 (hereafter *Letter to Tordoff*) also *Qq262, 266; Ev,,p294*

[311] *Q67; Ev, p27 paragraph 10, p48 section 5.3, pp214–5, p233 paragraph 6, p271 paragraph 4, pp286–95*

[312] *Ev, p245 section 3* and see *Q233*

[313] *Qq272, 274*

[314] *Letter to Tordoff* and *Q230; Ev, p264*

[315] *Letter to Tordoff*

120. Once it is established which law applies to transactions, consumers can face difficulties in obtaining effective redress. Application of the country of origin principle raises the unpalatable prospect for consumers of launching potentially costly legal actions in distant, foreign courts, using unfamiliar procedures. The National Consumer Council argued that "it is unrealistic to expect individual consumers to use resolution procedures in another country, possibly in a different language and based on an unfamiliar legal system".[316] The issue is further complicated by the existence of the Brussels and Lugano Conventions which are designed "to regulate civil and commercial disputes of a private nature between two parties in different states and to provide rules for the enforcement of judgements". These are under review and it has been suggested that they both should cover electronic contracts, possibly causing conflict with the provisions of the draft Directive.[317] It is not clear how these conventions, or the Rome Convention which establishes rules to determine which national laws should apply to contractual disputes, relate to the proposals made in the draft Electronic Commerce Directive.[318] The Directive places emphasis on voluntary arrangements to deal with redress, but these will clearly not be sufficient in every case.

121. The position with regard to consumer protection and redress is even less satisfactory when transactions take place between consumers in the UK and firms beyond the borders of the EU. The National Consumer Council said that "piecemeal initiatives" were being undertaken by OECD, the International Chambers of Commerce and others to draw up guidelines and codes of best practice relating to consumer protection in cross-border transactions, but these fall a long way short of formal procedures to protect consumers.[319] The NCC told us that "buyer beware" might be the most appropriate phrase to use in connection with electronic commerce, but this is hardly likely to encourage consumers to begin carrying out transactions on-line.[320]

122. The Government told us that "market solutions were developing which will go much of the way to giving consumers the confidence they need" including an "on-line digital hallmark" which was announced in the Competitiveness White Paper, and a recent Consumers Association initiative.[321] e centre$^{UK}$ mentioned the increasing importance of codes of practice on websites.[322] The National Consumer Council stressed the importance of such self-regulatory initiatives. It told us that "there are very few instances where consumers actually seek legal redress in relation to...normal consumer transactions. The key thing for us is to get it right at the beginning, to make sure the best practice information is established. That might be best done with self regulation".[323] Consumers in Europe Group warned that self-regulation required procedures to handle cross-border disputes; the National Consumer Council argued that there was a need for "clearing houses at a national level", to pursue cross-border redress issues on behalf of consumers.[324] Whatever procedures are devised should be based on the principle that consumers are entitled to have timely and affordable access to mechanisms of redress when transactions go wrong.

123. Consumers are already, at least partly, protected from mistakes and mishaps when they purchase goods on the internet using a credit card. Under section 75 of the Consumer Credit Act 1974, credit card companies and traders jointly hold equal liability for claims in the event of errors, over and above an excess.[325] Several witnesses argued that the Act applied only to domestic transactions and needed to be explicitly extended to cover international transactions.[326] We asked DTI to clarify the legal position. We were told that "the impact of section 75 on overseas transactions is unclear and has not been clarified by the courts. We have no evidence

---

[316] *Ev, p88 paragraph 5.6 and Q240*

[317] *Ev, p196 paragraph 4.13*; also *Ev, p277 annex A*; *Financial Times, 6 Jul 99*

[318] *Ev, p245 section 3*

[319] *Ev, p88 paragraph 5.2*; also *Ev, p54 Annex 1 paragraph A1.15*; *Consumer Protection in the Electronic Marketplace,* OECD, Oct 98, DSTI/CP(98)13/REV2 and *Draft Declaration on Consumer Protection in the Context of Electronic Commerce*, OECD, Oct 98, OECD DSTI/CP(98)12/REV2

[320] *Q230*

[321] *Ev, p195 paragraph 4.10 and see Ev, p88 paragraph 5.4*

[322] *Q43*; and see *Ev, p48 section 5.4*

[323] *Q222*

[324] *Qq235, 272; Ev, p88 paragraph 5.7 and p245 section 3*

[325] *Ev, p88, paragraph 4.5–4.8*

[326] *Qq226, 287–8; Ev, p88 paragraphs 4.7–4.8, p110 section 6*

that UK consumers are suffering any detriment at present and we have no plans to make any changes to the legislation".[327] It would appear that, although section 75 might not apply to overseas transactions, the credit card companies have voluntarily agreed to act as if it did and no case law exists to decide the issue. **We recommend that, if any court was to decide that section 75 of the Consumer Credit Act 1974 did not apply to overseas transactions, then DTI speedily bring forward legislation to fill the gap.**

124. **International agreement is essential to deal both with sharp practices and the legal questions of consumer protection and redress arising from electronic commerce. Even at EU level, agreement on how to deal with these question has not been reached and the situation is confused. This may not yet have hindered the development of electronic commerce, which has, so far, been focused mostly on relatively simple goods, such as books and CDs, which might rarely give rise to disputes between buyer and vendor. Electronic trade in more complex products is more likely to be deterred by uncertainties as to what protection exists for consumers when things go wrong. At the very least, consumers need to know what rights they have when they engage in on-line trade, and how those rights can be exercised. We would expect DTI's forthcoming consumer White Paper to deal with these issues.**

### Trade Policy

125. The Second Ministerial Council of the World Trade Organisation (WTO), at Geneva in May 1998, called for the initiation of a work programme to examine all trade related issues connected to electronic commerce.[328] Such a work programme was adopted in September 1998.[329] It included an examination of the treatment of electronic commerce in the General Agreement on Tariffs and Services, the General Agreement on Tariffs and Trade, the Agreement on Trade Related Aspects of Intellectual Property Rights and related agreements, as well as development aspects of electronic commerce. Final reports on each of these issues are due to be submitted to the WTO's General Council by 30 July 1999.[330]

126. The Government told us that "it is not yet clear as to whether there is a case for developing a discrete set of WTO rules on e-commerce" and that there was "a reasonably close approach between the EU and the US on most of the issues".[331] One issue does divide the EU and US: whether or not certain "goods" delivered over the internet, particularly those with similarities to physical goods — such as text which could be converted into a book — should be treated as services, and therefore subject to the General Agreement on Tariffs and Services, or treated similarly to physical goods.[332] **Neutrality between trade carried out on-line and off-line should be the key principle underpinning any future consideration of the relationship between electronic commerce and international trade rules.**

### Duty

127. The WTO's 1998 Ministerial Council also resolved that electronic transmissions should not be subject to customs duties. As a consequence, music downloaded from an internet site based overseas can be purchased duty-free, while the same music recorded on a compact disc or other device and sent physically would probably incur duty.[333] This offends against one of the principles relating to the taxation of electronic commerce, namely that taxation rules should apply equally to on-line as to off-line commerce.[334] As with sales taxes, such as VAT, the difficulty with applying customs duties to electronic transactions lies in their collection: data messages do not stop at national borders in order for duty to be levied. The next WTO Ministerial Council, at Seattle in November 1999, will review the application of customs duties

---

[327] Ev, p5 question 11

[328] *Declaration on Global Electronic Commerce*, WTO, 25 May 98, on the internet at www.wto.org/wto/ecom/e_mindec1.htm

[329] *Work Programme on Electronic Commerce*, WTO, 25 Sep 98, on the internet at www.wto.org/wto/ecom/e_gc.htm; for an analysis of WTO's work programme see *World Trade Agenda*, No. 99/2, 26 Apr 99, pp6–11

[330] *Ev, p329–330*

[331] *Ev, p330*

[332] *Ev, p330*

[333] Customs authorities can exempt from duty goods valued at below a certain limit

[334] Paragraph 101

to electronic transactions; we have heard no arguments to suggest that the 1998 resolution should be changed or that, if it were, customs duties on electronic transactions could be levied successfully.[335]

128. Customs duties are levied on goods ordered electronically, but delivered physically. The imposition of such duties, and the time taken for goods to pass through customs procedures, can have a significant impact on customers' perceptions of the benefits of electronic commerce. Overseas goods may appear to be cheaper than those sold domestically when shown on a website, but once customs duties and potentially unpredictable cross-border delays are taken into account the advantages of purchasing over the internet may seem rather limited.[336] HM Customs & Excise have provided a useful on-line guide to how much duty and VAT would be due on importations of a range of consumer goods.[337] The Government told us that "electronic commerce will generate a large increase in small volume importation by consumers and small and medium sized enterprises of goods ordered electronically from overseas suppliers".[338] Such an increase may exacerbate cross-border delays, and also provide incentives for some countries to alter their customs rules in order to raise more revenue from trade generated by electronic commerce. During our visit to the US we were told that the customs authorities there were now showing more interest in the import and export of small packages due to the growth of internet retail. **The potential benefits to consumers of buying cheaper goods from overseas using the internet might be lost if the duties levied and procedures followed by customs authorities fail to facilitate small cross-border transactions.**

129. The Government stated in its written evidence that electronic commerce can "provide a major contribution to rationalising and simplifying trade procedures worldwide for conventional shipments" which will benefit the UK and other industrialised countries, as well as generating "particular gains for developing countries".[339] e centre[UK] told us that "UK competitiveness requires further simplification and streamlining of trade procedures, especially customs procedures".[340] Within the UK, the Government cited the example of new procedures for applications for strategic export licenses, with which we dealt in our last Report on electronic commerce.[341] Internationally, the EU is pressing for trade facilitation issues to be included "prominently" in the next round of WTO trade negotiations.[342] We received details of several trade facilitation initiatives.[343] **We would support the inclusion of trade facilitation procedures on the agenda of the next round of multilateral trade negotiations.**

DEVELOPMENT

130. We have highlighted the potentially beneficial effects of electronic commerce on rural and remote areas of the UK and socially disadvantaged groups.[344] In both cases, traditional disadvantages — for example of location and mobility — can be overcome because electronic commerce may permit complex transactions to be undertaken without the parties involved needing to meet, and because the internet can make available a vast range of information to anyone with an appropriate telephone connection. These potential benefits of electronic commerce may also be applicable to developing economies. The primary constraint on the take-up of electronic commerce in developing countries at present is limited telecommunications infrastructure. This constraint could be overcome at a stroke by the advent of affordable mobile and satellite communications capable of facilitating internet connection, perhaps only a few

---

[335] The US Secretary of Commerce recently stated that "internet must be a duty-free zone, no ifs, ands or buts" — to the Opening Plenary Session of the Industrial Sector Advisory Committees, Washington DC, 11 Jun 99, on the internet at 204.193.246.62/public.nsf/docs/990616-committees-opening-plenary-session-dc

[336] *Ev, p262*

[337] On the internet atwww.hmce.gov.uk/general/question/index.htm

[338] *Ev, p199 paragraph 4.47*

[339] *Ibid*

[340] *Ev, p5 section 14*

[341] *Paragraphs 57, 111–2; Ev, p199 paragraph 4.48*

[342] *Ev, p199 paragraph 4.47*

[343] *Ev, p5 section 14, p107 and DTI press notice, 99/23, 14 Jan 99; United Nations Economic Commission for Europe, Press notice, ECE/TRADE/99/4, 17 Mar 99 about the recent International Seminar on Trade Facilitation and Electronic Business; and see World Trade Agenda, No. 99/1, 9 Mar 99, pp13–14*

[344] Paragraph 47

years away.[345] Although the potential impact of electronic commerce on developing countries is part of the current WTO work programme, there is little work being done on this subject in other fora.[346] **We recommend that the Department for International Development consider the contribution the UK can make to ensuring that developing countries benefit from the opportunities offered by electronic commerce.**

### Privacy

131. Electronic commerce is introducing new ways in which personal data can be communicated and collected. Electronic mail provides a new means by which people can be contacted; visits to websites can be monitored, and visitors' data collected, by software known as "cookies"; websites can deny access to visitors who have not previously registered their personal details with the firms that maintain them; similar registration procedures are often necessary before transactions can be conducted on-line; and personal information can be made available on newsgroups.[347] The Data Protection Registrar told us that "although the application of the technologies involved in e-commerce are new the data protection issues which arise are not".[348] The provisions of the Data Protection Acts 1984 and 1998 apply to the processing of personal data on-line as much as off-line.[349] Users should be clearly notified of what personal data is being collected from them and what might be done with that information; under the provisions of the 1998 Act, which is not yet in force,[350] data processors will need to demonstrate that they have legitimate grounds for collecting personal information.[351]

132. As the Data Protection Registrar pointed out in her written memorandum, "the nature of electronic commerce makes it easier for organisations collecting information via websites to provide effective notifications to the individual" about their data collection practices. Many websites contain privacy statements or automatically notify users that information is being collected, and for what purpose. The Data Protection Registrar has supported the OECD in the development of guidelines for organisations designing privacy policies and statements.[352] The infringement of data protection regulations can be difficult to detect, however, not least because of the ease with which data can be collected surreptitiously on-line.[353] Technology can work both for and against the protection of individuals' privacy in relation to electronic commerce. Some internet browsers can automatically detect and disable surreptitious data collection when individuals visit websites, although this might not stop such data collection occurring by other means. On the other hand, we heard of two recent cases of computer hardware and software being produced with unique serial numbers which might effectively prevent their users from remaining anonymous when engaged in electronic commerce.[354]

133. Privacy is a sensitive issue with consumers, particularly with those new to computer technology and electronic commerce. The Data Protection Registrar indicated that consumers would be deterred from undertaking electronic transactions if they were unsure of who had access to their data and how it might be used.[355] Privacy is closely related to security, the issue consistently identified by consumers and small and medium sized enterprise as their biggest concern about electronic commerce and use of the internet.[356] In our first Report on electronic

---

[345] Paragraph 48 and Ev, p143 paragraph 68

[346] The United Nations Conference on Trade and Development and the International Telecommunications Union have launched initiatives aimed at promoting electronic commerce in developing countries — see *Telecommunications Regulatory Issues for Electronic Commerce,* Report to the International Telecommunications Union 8th Regulatory Colloquium, Feb 99, p13; and see *Financial Times,* 30 Apr 98, p5 and *Sunday Business,* 15 Nov 98, p9

[347] *Q237; Ev, pp171–2 paragraph 12*

[348] *Ev, p171 paragraph 6*

[349] *Q465; Ev, p171 paragraphs 6, 11*

[350] The Act is due to come into force on 1 March 2000, see HC Deb, 12 Jul 99, c73w

[351] *Ev, p171 paragraphs 7–8, 11*

[352] *Ev, p171 paragraphs 8, 10* and see *Qq238, 464*

[353] *Ev, p171 paragraph 10*

[354] On the Intel Pentium III chip controversy see *Qq476, 513* and *Ev, pp174 paragraph 25, 306–7* and *Report on the Intel Pentium III Processor Serial Number Feature,* Cyber-Rights and Cyber-Liberties (UK), Feb99, on the internet at www.cyber-rights.org/reports/intel-rep./htm; on the Microsoft Windows 98 case see *Ev, pp306–7*

[355] *Ev, p172 paragraph 13*

[356] For a recent Government survey see *Electronic Government: The View from the Queue: Introduction,* Central Information Technology Unit, Oct 98, paragraphs 37–8

commerce we dealt at length with the implications for law enforcement agencies and others of the increasing availability and use of encryption technology.[357] We heard the views of the Data Protection Registrar on the interaction between the security and privacy debates and were also informed of the efforts of Cyber-Rights and Cyber-Liberties (UK) to ensure that internet service providers establish privacy policies to govern their dealings with the law enforcement agencies.[358]

134. There is a delicate balance to be drawn between the need to protect the security of on-line transactions, including the privacy of the personal information communicated, and to allow law enforcement agencies access to data which might be valuable evidence in criminal prosecutions. In our last Report we indicated that the Government's encryption policy had tended to favour law enforcement interests at the expense of the security and privacy of on-line transactions. Although the Data Protection Registrar contributed to the debate of the Government's encryption policy proposals, we received the impression that she had been somewhat overlooked by DTI while those proposals had been discussed within Government.[359] **We believe that the Data Protection Registrar has a vital role to play in ensuring that consumers understand what their rights are in relation to data protection,[360] and in monitoring market, policy and technological developments to warn and advise of changes which might encourage data protection infringements. We recommend that the Registrar make use of her powers to report to Parliament where necessary to draw attention to such developments. The Registrar's expertise on data protection issues should be exploited to the full by the Government while it is considering its policy proposals. As information increasingly becomes a key generator of economic growth and prosperity, the Data Protection Registrar's role will become ever more important. The Government must ensure that the Registrar has all the resources she requires to deal with the challenges she faces.[361]**

GLOBAL DATA PROTECTION

135. While data protection standards are defined by statute in Europe, self-regulation and voluntary codes of conduct protect privacy on-line in the United States. Progress in introducing robust self-regulatory mechanisms has been slow, leading to a dispute between the US and the EU over cross-border information flows.[362] Principle 8 of the Data Protection Act 1998, which will implement the EU Data Protection Directive of 1995, "restricts the transfer of personal data to countries and territories outside the European Economic Area unless the third country can provide adequate safeguards for the data". The Act covers material placed on the internet but does not prevent information flows "with the consent of the consumer" or where necessary for the performance of a contract. The extent to which a safeguard is adequate will depend on "the circumstances in a particular case, such as the final destination of the data or whether or not the data is sensitive". The Data Protection Registrar told us that this provision "should mean that consumers are able to maintain some control over the final destination of their data". [363]

136. The Management Consultancies Association warned us that the new European data protection regime could cause uncertainties about the transfer of information abroad which might "constitute a major entry barrier particularly for small and medium sized enterprises wishing to enter the e-commerce market either in the UK or the rest of the EC". The Association also criticised the cumbersome nature of the procedures firms would be required to use in order to ensure that transfers abroad were legal.[364] The Data Protection Registrar challenged this interpretation of the implications of the legislation. She argued that any problems encountered by firms could be "readily solved by clearly telling individuals what will happen to their data and

---

[357] especially *paragraphs 9–37, 80–110*

[358] *Qq483–4, 487, 508–9; Ev, p172 paragraphs 15–18, p186 paragraphs 25–29*

[359] *Qq 484, 487*

[360] *Ev, pp174–5 paragraph 28 and Q464*

[361] *Qq467–75*

[362] *Qq268, 477; Ev, p53 annex 1 paragraph A1.1, pp234–5, 244 section 2, p249 paragraph 10; Application of a Methodology Designed to Assess the Adequacy of the Level of Protection of Individuals with regard to Processing Personal Data: test of the method of several categories of transfer*, paper prepared for the European Commission by Charles D. Raab et al, Edinburgh University, Sep 98, p164 paragraphs 32–4. The paper also covers personal data protection in Australia, Canada, New Zealand, Japan and Hong Kong

[363] *Ev, p173 paragraph 21*

[364] *Ev, p215 section 1*

obtaining their agreement." This can be done on-line and we were told of initiatives underway to establish easy ways of publishing privacy statements on websites. The Registrar said that she would issue guidance on this issue shortly.[365] The European Commission has sought to reach an arrangement with the US Department of Commerce to reduce uncertainty about the circumstances in which data transfers to the US might infringe EU legislation, by the formulation of guidelines to US organisations — the Safe Harbor principles. These are likely to be finalised in the autumn.[366] The Data Protection Registrar warned that the Safe Harbor principles might not be able to guarantee that all data flows from the EU to the US meet EU data protection standards and that this would be something "we are going to have to keep an eye on".[367]

137. The fear of files of personal information being secretly collated on computer databases around the world, and then being used by Governments and big businesses, often lies at the heart of that suspicion and distrust of computerisation which exists. The Data Protection Registrar, and her European colleagues, are rightly concerned with combatting that fear by preventing firms abusing the personal information they receive from consumers. **Protection of consumers' data, like the protection of their health and legal rights, must be vigorously defended by Government. Infringements of data protection standards cannot be excused by doubtful arguments that such standards are too expensive or complicated to defend.**

## VII CONCLUSION

138. **We believe that electronic commerce could have a major impact on the UK economy. The Government is right to identify the need for the UK to become an attractive place to conduct electronic transactions, in order for the international competitiveness of the UK economy to be maintained and improved. We have criticised some of the measures proposed by Government which, in our opinion, might undermine the UK's competitiveness — for instance, in relation to encryption and authentication, both covered in our previous Report on electronic commerce — and we are also concerned at the lack of urgency in some aspects of policy, including the continuing delays in the publication of the Electronic Commerce Bill and the appointment of the e-Envoy. Nevertheless, our overall assessment is that, in terms of the economic aspects of electronic commerce, the Government is slowly moving in the right direction.**

139. **Aside from economic issues, this Report has considered other dimensions of the electronic commerce debate. Social issues relating to electronic commerce have perhaps been eclipsed by the important, but not over-riding, concerns of industry and law enforcement. We think it imperative that all sections of society share in the potential benefits of electronic commerce — there needs to be increased attention paid by Government to access, skills and consumer protection issues in order to facilitate the achievement of this objective. We have also examined the way in which Government is structured to deal with the issues arising from electronic commerce. It is important that the Government resist the temptation to intervene in relation to every issue arising from electronic commerce but, equally, the Government, especially DTI, should seek to build and retain its capacity to deal with the problems and challenges likely to emerge swiftly and sometimes unexpectedly in this area in future.**

---

[365] *Q494; Ev, pp308–9, section 3*; and paragraph 132
[366] See Joint Report on Data Protection Dialogue to the EU/US Summit, 21 June 1999, on the internet at www.ita.doc.gov/ecom/jointreport2617.htm; but see *Financial Times*, 16 Jun 99, p6
[367] *Q478; Ev, p174 paragraphs 23–4*

# SUMMARY OF CONCLUSIONS AND RECOMMENDATIONS

*Overall Conclusions*

(a) **It is important that, when considering how best the Government should respond to the growth of electronic commerce, potential advantages and disadvantages of the phenomenon are kept in perspective. Policy makers must be careful not to be carried away by the hyperbole and exaggeration which has, at times, come to characterise the debate on the future development of electronic commerce. Nor should their focus stray from those aspects of society which are unlikely to be touched by electronic commerce or which may be in some way damaged by it. Electronic commerce must not be regarded as a panacea for every difficult issue facing politicians today nor as the issue which most firms and individuals will believe to be most relevant to their daily lives. Nevertheless, DTI, perhaps more than any other Government department, must increasingly seek to promote the positive benefits of electronic commerce, particularly in terms of its potential impact on UK competitiveness, and at the same time seek to alleviate its drawbacks. In considering how best to respond to the new challenges posed by electronic commerce, the Government must pay particular attention to those areas from which it should hold back from intervening (paragraphs 9, 10 and 20).**

(b) **Electronic commerce is eroding national, and regional, boundaries in many different policy areas. It has the potential to change relationships within Government and between Government and society at large as well as to alter many public policy perspectives (paragraphs 21 and 100).**

*Measuring Electronic Commerce*

(c) **We recommend that the Government consider how electronic commerce should be defined, in order to facilitate comparison between the growth of electronic commerce in the UK and abroad. We recommend that the Government Statistical Service consider how best to develop new statistical measures relating to electronic commerce and to adopt its existing measures to the phenomenon (paragraphs 11 and 13).**

(d) **DTI are to be congratulated for the efforts they have made to ensure that the performance of UK businesses, in terms of information and communications technology usage, can be measured alongside that of other major economies. The results show that the UK is in a strong position to be at the forefront of the development of electronic commerce. There can be no room for complacency, however, and clear problems have been shown up. Very small businesses and some 'traditional' industrial sectors have not kept pace with their international competitors in this area and this may have a detrimental impact on the competitiveness of the UK economy in the years ahead. Government policy must focus on these firms and on those regions in which take-up of new information and communications technologies has been sluggish. The Regional Development Agencies and devolved bodies may have an important role to play in this regard. Numerical indicators, for instance of the number of firms on-line, are not necessarily the best or only measures of the quality of the UK's environment for electronic trading. We suggest that the UK's legislative and regulatory framework, which the Information Age Partnership highlighted as an area of relative strength, should be taken into account when measuring the merits of that environment. The conclusions and recommendations we make in this Report, and those from our previous Report on electronic commerce, are intended to strengthen that framework and to help the Government achieve its ambitious aim for the UK to become the best environment for electronic trading by 2002 (paragraphs 18 and 19).**

*Structure of Government*

(e)   We do not think that the creation of a new unit or division within Government exclusively concerned with electronic commerce would be a useful innovation, or something welcomed by industry. Nor do we believe that it would necessarily be helpful at this stage to tinker with the division of responsibilities for electronic commerce policy between departments and agencies or to create new cross-departmental structures. Getting the policies right is more important (paragraph 25).

(f)   We note the work commenced by OFTEL to tackle the electronic commerce policy agenda, including issues well beyond those relating to authentication and encryption for which the Director General of Telecommunications might soon have statutory responsibility. OFTEL's electronic commerce team must quickly establish a cooperative relationship with the e-Envoy, when appointed, in order to ensure that their respective remits are appropriately coordinated (paragraph 28).

(g)   We recommend that the Director General of Telecommunications be given a specific duty to facilitate electronic commerce, at the earliest opportunity. We would expect the Director General, in response, to publish a statement of how he intends to comply with his new duty (paragraph 31).

*The e-Envoy*

(h)   We would welcome the appointment of an e-Envoy. The e-Envoy could be an effective ambassador for electronic commerce in the UK, an international ambassador for the UK as a centre of digital excellence and an advocate within Government for the policies and initiatives required for the UK to become the world's best environment for electronic trading. The appointment of a high-calibre, dynamic individual as e-Envoy could represent a high profile commitment by Government to electronic commerce, the like of which has so far been lacking. Perceptions of the independence from Government of the e-Envoy are likely to be enhanced if it is made clear that the post-holder is not a civil servant. In order to be effective, the e-Envoy must not be seen within Government as a DTI official, defending the department's line on issues which cut across departmental boundaries.

(i)   It is vital that the Government, in consultation with the post-holder, devises and publishes the objectives of the e-Envoy and the resources which will be available to the e-Envoy to achieve those objectives. Progress made by the e-Envoy towards the achievement of his or her objectives should be assessed by means of measurable targets, drawn up by the Government. We would expect the e-Envoy to publish regular reports to Parliament detailing progress made towards the achievement of his or her objectives, difficulties and obstacles met, and future targets set (paragraphs 32, 33, 34 and 36).

(j)   Ministers must not seek to burden the e-Envoy with a host of unduly ambitious and unrealistic objectives and responsibilities. The role of e-Envoy will be discredited if it is seen to combine responsibility without power. Ministers must define the policy framework within which the e-Envoy will work, rather than deflect difficult decisions and thorny issues towards a prominent but unempowered official (paragraph 35).

(k)   We see merit in the appointment of the proposed Government/industry forum on encryption and believe that it is essential that the e-Envoy participate in it. (Paragraph 37).

(l)   The delay in appointing the e-Envoy, as yet unexplained, has not served to demonstrate the strength of the Government's commitment to the role or to the need for urgent policy initiatives on electronic commerce. It would seem to suggest, instead, that electronic commerce was not a priority of Government. We recommend that this impression be dispelled by an appointment at the earliest opportunity, so that the successful candidate can start making up for lost time. (Paragraph 38).

*Using the Internet: Infrastructure*

(m) We agree with OFTEL that BT's monopoly ownership and control of the local loop could restrict the roll-out of vital new high-bandwidth services. Although OFTEL has no role to play in championing the development of particular technologies — such as DSL — we believe that it must be proactive in ensuring that competitive forces exert their influence throughout the UK's telecommunications infrastructure so that residential consumers and small and medium sized enterprises can benefit from a choice of high-bandwidth technologies from different operators (paragraph 46).

(n) Electronic commerce offers the opportunity to unlock the potential of the rural economy. The Government must ensure that this opportunity is exploited, not wasted due to deficiencies in the nation's telecommunications infrastructure, by ensuring that there exists effective competition in the supply of high-bandwidth services to all users, not just those in urban or suburban areas (paragraph 47).

*Using the Internet: Cost*

(o) For most residential customers and SMEs using the internet local telephone charges are the marginal cost of going on-line and, as such, are a key influence over the extent to which such consumers and enterprises engage in electronic commerce. The possibility of receiving a substantial telephone bill as a result of regular use of the internet, and the widespread perception of this occurring, seem to us to be obvious disincentives to greater use of the internet and, therefore, participation in electronic commerce (paragraphs 51 and 58).

(p) The more widespread availability to residential customers of unmetered local telephone calls would give electronic commerce in the UK a substantial boost. We judge that OFTEL has been unduly cautious in emphasising the possible disadvantages of unmetered local calls, at the expense of the potential benefits. In line with our recommendation that the Director General of Telecommunication be given a duty to facilitate electronic commerce, we recommend that OFTEL investigates what, if any, regulatory actions are required to encourage innovative tariff packages being offered to internet users throughout the UK; and devote resources to studying and publicising the comparative costs of internet access packages, in order to dispel the seemingly widespread perception that anything more than a cursory use of the internet would prove prohibitively expensive (paragraph 59).

(q) We welcome OFTEL's recognition that consumers need full and clear information about the tariffs charged by different telephone operators in order for them to take full advantage of the opportunities offered by competition in the telecommunications market. Urgent progress in this area is now required (paragraph 53).

(r) Without high-bandwidth services, in particular leased lines, UK businesses will be unable to offer effective and innovative electronic services, resulting in their competitive advantages being ceded to foreign rivals. Ensuring that UK firms have a choice of competitively-priced high-quality high-bandwidth services must be an urgent priority for OFTEL. We support the Government in its efforts to focus the attention of the European Commission on the need to ensure that European leased lines prices are competitive with those offered in the US (paragraphs 64 and 65).

(s) We welcome the work being undertaken by DTI to compare the prices of consumer goods in the UK and elsewhere and hope that it will be followed by swift action to ensure that British consumers fully benefit from competition in the computer hardware market (paragraph 66).

*Social Exclusion Issues*

(t)   Personal computers, the internet and electronic commerce should not be seen as exclusively playthings of the middle classes. We want to see everyone in society — rich or poor, young or old — able to take part in and benefit from electronic commerce. It will be a measure of the Government's success if, in five years time, the profile of the average internet user more closely resembles the population as a whole rather than being skewed towards young, university-educated men. Aside from considerations of social justice and equity, widespread take-up of electronic commerce could provide immense benefits to British industry as well as cost savings for Government. We are of the impression that the Government shares our objective, but we think some more vocal advocacy and more dynamic policies, particularly in relation to socially disadvantaged groups, are called for. We recommend that Ministers, and the e-Envoy once appointed, give a lead in democratising and demystifying electronic commerce (paragraph 75).

(u)   The Government should examine how consumers without bank accounts can be encouraged to participate in electronic commerce (paragraph 69).

(v)   One of the burgeoning number of units within DTI might be well placed to research the implications for UK employment of the growth of electronic commerce, and we recommend that such research is carried out (paragraph 76).

(w)   We recommend that the Government begin a national debate about how the universal service concept can be applied to electronic commerce (paragraph 80).

*Business Support*

(x)   There will need to be a step change in the attitude of very small firms to the use of external communications technologies in order for the UK to catch up with the best of the G7 in this area. Although it is not easy to tell how many firms are currently buying and selling on-line, the target of having 1 million small and medium sized enterprises buying and selling on-line by 2002 will be significantly more difficult to achieve than that of having 1 million such firms regularly using information and communications technology by that date (paragraph 82).

(y)   There is a danger that the projects outlined in the Competitiveness White Paper are not capable of making a significant contribution towards the achievement of the ambitious goals set out by the Government in relation to the participation of small and medium sized enterprises in electronic commerce. Too many of the initiatives seem ill-thought out and lacking in detail — promising on paper, but, so far, short of substance. There is a worrying lack of attention to the coordination of these projects with existing initiatives, the proposed Small Business Service, new regional organisations and the devolved Assemblies. We recommend that DTI publish details of progress made in implementing those initiatives relating to electronic commerce launched in the Competitiveness White Paper, how those initiatives are to be coordinated with regional and national bodies including the proposed Small Business Service, and how they will be evaluated in further Implementation Plans (paragraph 86).

(z)   Small businesses remain unpersuaded of the usefulness of Business Link services, including Local Support Centres, as providers of advice on electronic commerce. We are not convinced that it is desirable for the Government to sponsor the provision of advice on information and communications technology to firms through a hotch-potch of seemingly unrelated organisations. A greater degree of national consistency is required. We recommend that steps are taken to improve the consistency and coordination of the electronic commerce support services offered to small and medium sized enterprises, including clarification of the relationship between Local Support Centres and the proposed Small Business Service (paragraphs 89 and 90).

(aa) **We welcome the increasing use made of the internet to provide business support services. DTI should ensure that its on-line services are coordinated with the business support services it sponsors off-line. Particularly given the frequency with which new laws refers back to older pieces of legislation, we recommend that the Government consider placing all primary and secondary legislation currently in force on-line (paragraphs 91 and 92).**

*Eectronic Government*

(bb) **CITU's analysis shows that most Departments already provide more than 25% of their services by volume electronically. The 2002 target is therefore not particularly challenging, although the 2008 target might prove a challenge to some departments. However, making a service available electronically is no guarantee that anyone will wish to use it in that way; it is essential that the electronic Government agenda is driven by the needs and requirements of users, not by what Government officials assume these to be; and high-profile failures to implement electronic Government projects send out the wrong signals to the private sector about the potential attractions and benefits of electronic commerce (paragraph 95).**

(cc) **We are concerned that the electronic Government agenda is characterised by hyperbole, over-optimism about the capabilities of management to implement novel technological systems on a large scale, and repeated failures to learn from past mistakes. There is an urgent need for a hard-headed assessment, across Government, of what electronic services are required by users and how these best can be delivered and financed. However desirable and convenient they may be in theory, ambitious cross-departmental projects and "one-stop-shops" are of no use to man nor beast unless they can be delivered on time, in budget, and in full working order. The current plague of costly, late and untested electronic Government projects must be tackled before the situation worsens (paragraph 96).**

(dd) **Care must be taken to ensure that those who cannot use new technologies, or those who, for whatever reasons, choose not to do so, are not discriminated against because of the rush to embrace electronic commerce (paragraph 97).**

(ee) **DTI should seek to ensure that its websites remain up-to-date, well organised and operative in order so that they become an increasingly important means of disseminating information and facilitating contact with the public. (Paragraph 99).**

*Taxation*

(ff) **We welcome the Government's indication that it will play an active role in the international efforts to safeguard national taxation revenues from a proliferation of low-tax or tax-free internet gambling facilities (paragraph 104).**

(gg) **The world's major economies broadly agree on the principles which should underpin the taxation of electronic commerce. Rapid progress in reaching agreement on how the international tax system should be adjusted to take account of electronic commerce is unlikely, however. The issues are not only complicated but, especially in relation to sales taxes, solutions are hoped for rather than expected to be found. There is also a danger that the broad principles which it is agreed should underpin the taxation of electronic commerce might be undermined by compromises and agreements reached on issues which, although minor in themselves, have unintended and unwelcome cumulative effects. The slow pace of policy development might prove advantageous, in that it could ensure any agreement reached is not overtaken by technological developments or unforeseen consumer trends. We would welcome frequent updates from the UK tax authorities on progress made on reaching international agreements in this area. (Paragraph 106).**

*Intellectual Property Rights*

(hh)  We welcome the Government's commitment to ensuring that a "fair balance is achieved between rights holders and users": once that has been achieved at European level it must be swiftly transposed into UK law in order to clarify the present legal position in several vital areas. We welcome the swift progress made in resolving tensions between the EU and US concerning the allocation of domain names (paragraphs 110 and 114).

*Consumer Protection*

(ii)  In many respects, transactions which make use of a computer are no different from mail-order or telephone transactions. Electronic commerce transactions, although often carried out in a consumer's home or work place, might have the same legal status as transactions made abroad, for instance when a consumer is on holiday, as a result of the implementation of the draft EU Legal Aspects of Electronic Commerce Directive. It is vital that, when buying on the internet, consumers are made fully aware of the jurisdiction under which the transaction is taking place. The development of a single EU electronic commerce market is likely to increase pressure for the harmonisation of consumer protection legislation. Such harmonisation must not involve any reduction in the level of protection currently offered to consumers by UK legislation (paragraph 119).

(jj)  We recommend that, if any court was to decide that section 75 of the Consumer Credit Act 1974 did not apply to overseas transactions, then DTI speedily bring forward legislation to fill the gap (paragraph 123).

(kk)  International agreement is essential to deal both with sharp practices and the legal questions of consumer protection and redress arising from electronic commerce. Even at EU level, agreement on how to deal with these question has not been reached and the situation is confused. This may not yet have hindered the development of electronic commerce, which has, so far, been focused mostly on relatively simple goods, such as books and CDs, which might rarely give rise to disputes between buyer and vendor. Electronic trade in more complex products is more likely to be deterred by uncertainties as to what protection exists for consumers when things go wrong. At the very least, consumers need to know what rights they have when they engage in on-line trade, and how those rights can be exercised. We would expect DTI's forthcoming consumer White Paper to deal with these issues (paragraph 124).

*Trade Issues*

(ll)  Neutrality between trade carried out on-line and off-line should be the key principle underpinning any future consideration of the relationship between electronic commerce and international trade rules (paragraph 126).

(mm) The potential benefits to consumers of buying cheaper goods from overseas using the internet might be lost if the duties levied and procedures followed by customs authorities fail to facilitate small cross-border transactions. We would support the inclusion of trade facilitation procedures on the agenda of the next round of multilateral trade negotiations (paragraph 129).

*Development*

(nn)  We recommend that the Department for International Development consider the contribution the UK can make to ensuring that developing countries benefit from the opportunities offered by electronic commerce. (Paragraph 130).

*Privacy*

(oo)  Protection of consumers' data, like the protection of their health and legal rights, must be vigorously defended by Government. Infringements of data protection standards cannot be excused by doubtful arguments that such standards are too expensive or complicated to defend (paragraph 137).

(pp) We believe that the Data Protection Registrar has a vital role to play in ensuring that consumers understand what their rights are in relation to data protection, and in monitoring market, policy and technological developments to warn and advise of changes which might encourage data protection infringements. We recommend that the Registrar make use of her powers to report to Parliament where necessary to draw attention to such developments. The Registrar's expertise on data protection issues should be exploited to the full by the Government while it is considering its policy proposals. As information increasingly becomes a key generator of economic growth and prosperity, the Data Protection Registrar's role will become ever more important. The Government must ensure that the Registrar has all the resources she requires to deal with the challenges she faces. The Government has a duty to set the highest standards of data protection in its own electronic commerce projects (paragraphs 98 and 134).

## MINUTES OF PROCEEDINGS
## RELATING TO THE REPORT

### THURSDAY 15 JULY 1999

Members present:

Mr Martin O'Neill, in the Chair

| | |
|---|---|
| Mr Tony Baldry | Mr Alasdair Morgan |
| Mr Roger Berry | Mrs Linda Perham |
| Mr Lindsay Hoyle | Mrs Helen Southworth |
| Mr Bob Laxton | |

The Committee deliberated.

Draft Report (Electronic Commerce), proposed by the Chairman, brought up and read.

*Ordered,* That the Report be read a second time, paragraph by paragraph.

Paragraphs 1 to 139 read and agreed to.

*Resolved,* That the Report be the Tenth Report of the Committee to the House.

*Ordered,* That the Chairman do make the Report to the House.

*Ordered,* That the provisions of Standing Order No. 134 (Select committees (reports)) be applied to the Report.

Several papers were ordered to be appended to the Report.

*Ordered,* That the Appendices to the Report be reported to the House.

[Adjourned till Tuesday 14 September
at Eleven o'clock

# LIST OF WITNESSES

# LIST OF MEMORANDA INCLUDED IN
# THE MINUTES OF EVIDENCE
(HC 187)

*Page*

*Submitted by*

# LIST OF APPENDICES TO THE
# MINUTES OF EVIDENCE
### (HC 187)

*Page*

*Submitted by*

# APPENDICES TO THE REPORT

## APPENDIX 1

**Memorandum submitted by The Department of Trade and Industry**

ANSWERS TO SUPPLEMENTARY QUESTIONS

COMPETITIVENESS WHITE PAPER

3. *Can you provide the Committee with a breakdown of how the £20 million extra funding over three years on connecting SMEs to the digital market place will be spent? Furthermore it would be useful to have further details of the following schemes and initiatives, particularly DTI's involvement with them, including financial and manpower commitments*

Individual funding allocations over the three year period covered by the Competiveness White Paper have not yet been made.

a. Adviser Skills Initiative

DTI's financial commitment last financial year was just over £250 thousand, with the four sponsor companies also each putting in £250 thousand.

    b. "New fund for partnership action to increase use of ICTs at local level and through supply chains" *(CWP, Implementation Plan, D3.5).*

    c. Local Partnership Fund.

    d. Sectoral/supply chain ICT development seminars.

    [b, c and d answered together]

        "New fund for partnership action" and the "Local Partnership Fund" are the same proposal. This will be developed with the emerging RDAs in England and the Scottish office, Welsh Office and Northern Ireland Office and the new Small Business Service. Similarly, the work on supply chains is at an early stage and requires development with new regional partners. No specific financial commitment has yet been made for this work.

e. E-commerce Resource Centre

Proposals for the E-Commerce Resource Centre are currently being considered with a view to providing an effective and good value for money alternative to developing the Centre from scratch (for which we originally envisaged a pump priming contribution of £200 thousand, with industry partners contributing on the design and development of the Centre).

f. Digital Business Awards

The E-Commerce Business Awards were launched in March. The first regional round of winners will be announced later this month with the national award to be announced on 17 June. DTI has been working with the Interforum group of companies to set up this initiative.

4. *It would be helpful to receive any assessment the Government may have commissioned of how many firms have used existing ISI Local Support Centres; the services they have received from such Centres; and the feedback received on the quality of such Centres; and also any plans the Government may have to commission such research in the future*

60,000 businesses used LSCs over the last 12 months and the numbers are rising. The LSCs provide a large range of services, tailored to individual local need, which cover one-to-one advice on e-commerce opportunities and provision of training, seminars and workshops. LSCs are also encouraged to develop local partnerships with further education colleges, universities and private sector IT suppliers. Monitoring and evaluation is undertaken at a number of levels:

    — Each LSC provides monitoring reports at six monthly intervals. Customer satisfaction rates reported are 85 per cent plus.

    — As the LSCs are all embedded in the existing SME support infrastructure, they are evaluated as part of the evalutation of their parent organisations—eg Business Links (BLs) in England. Management information on BL activity is collected and published quarterly. From July 1999, information will be collected, analysed and published on the impact that BL services (including LSCs) have on the profitability, turnover, productivity and export performance of assisted companies.

— We also monitor and evaluate the quality of LSCs by self assessment benchmarking tool. This has been developed to enable each LSC to identify its strengths and weaknesses against a number of factors that are considered critical to their success. The results from each LSC are analysed centrally and used to identify best practice and weak areas of performance that need attention.

— Finally, we are about to start an internal economic evaluation of the ISI which will include a focus on LSCs.

ACCESS ISSUES

6. *The Minister mentioned a communications strategy relating to electronic commerce (Q581); it would be useful to have some further information about the aims of this strategy, issues likely to be covered by it, and an indication of the date of publication*

An internal media strategy has been drawn up to promote ISI activities. Its aim is to fully exploit any newsworthy events to achieve sustained media coverage which will help meet the CWP commitments of the ISI programmes. Specifically these commitments are:

— to encourage greater SME use of ICTs;

— to encourage greater consumer use, by expanding the IT for All programme, by working with Business in the Community;

— to help UK businesses secure well over £300 million from EU content and application stimulation programmes.

Overall these targets will help meet the overarching Competitiveness White Paper target for making the UK the best environment in the world for electronic trading.

The ISI communications strategy is an internal working document and there are no plans to publish it.

7. *It would be helpful to receive some further details of the "Computers for All" initiative launched by the Chancellor of the Exchequer in his Budget speech, including funding arrangements and timetable for implementation (HC DBE, 9 Mar 99, c180)*

The £400 million package in England to improve access to ICT comprises three major schemes run by DfEE.

— A network of up to 800 IT Community Learning Centres in England. They will be situated in a range of schools, colleges, libraries and business locations, with 80 in inner-city areas as part of the DfEE's Excellence in Cities programme. Their focus will be on developing partnerships with business to meet the skills of tomorrow by bringing state-of-the-art ICT systems within the reach of everyone. The network will also support the University for Industry.

— A new co-ordinating group is being set up to steer the learning centres initiative and ensure effective co-operation with the University for Industry, the National Grid for Learning, the New Opportunities Fund, IT Centres of Excellence, the EU ADAPT initiative, DTI's IT programmes and other IT learning centre initiatives. It is expected that the group will have a private sector chair and membership, and include senior officials from DTI, DfEE and DCMS.

— A scheme for the refurbishment of computers which will be made available to low income families. The scheme will pilot lease arrangements to enable low income families to acquire low value or reconditioned computers for use in the home for homework and lifelong learning. Details of the scheme and eligibility criteria are in preparation.

— A scheme for subsidised loans to teachers for the purchase of computers at home. The aim is to provide improved or cheaper access to IT. Details of this scheme are also in preparation.

ELECTRONIC GOVERNMENT

8. *The Committee would be assisted by a memorandum on DTI's contribution to the Government's targets of 25 per cent of Government services on-line by 2002 and 90 per cent of routine procurement handles electronically by 2001, including an indication of the progress made to date, and information on progress in ensuring that import and export procedures can be completed electronically (CWP, Implementation Plan, D10.6)*

Twenty-five per cent and 90 per cent targets: The DTI fully expects to meet Prime Minister's target that, by 2002, 25 per cent of dealings with Government should be capable of being done by the public electronically. In volume terms, the bulk of the public's dealings with the DTI are carried out through Companies House, the Patent Office and the Radiocommunications Agency. About nine million individual transactions are carried out annually through these three agencies, accounting for more than 90 per cent of the Department's transactions with the public. Currently around 20 per cent of these transactions are capable of being conducted electronically.

By 2002 it is expected that about 80 per cent of services (by volume of transactions) will be available on-line, though the percentage take-up will be less, probably around 50 per cent. It is intended, for example, that by 2002 it will be possible to file returns at Companies House electronically.

The DTI's contract with the Unitas consortium (ICL and CMG) has established a public/private partnership aimed at successfully deploying information and communication technologies in support of electronic government. The primary driver for this is a three year programme of administrative process re-engineering projects examining areas such as electronic commerce and knowledge management. In respect of the target that by March 2001, 90 per cent by value of low value purchases by central government will be carried out electronically, the DTI is currently looking closely at four areas. These are:

— Our stationery contract with Niceday. Currently we are using the Government procurement Card for payment purposes on this contract. A further trial will involve us in examining a range of options with Niceday so that we can order from their electronic catalogue.

— Our travel contract with Carlson Wagonlit. This is being reviewed to see how we can transact with them electronically.

— Our contract with Expotel for hotel bookings. Again, we are looking to see how we can transact with them electronically.

— With Unitas—our IT providers—full electronic trading for ELGAR services is actively under review.

DTI is also developing the use of the Government Procurement Card. It is currently being piloted in three Directorates. We intend to roll it out to the whole Department during this year.

Taken together, these initiatives should account for much of our low value procurement, and will represent significant progress towards the 90 per cent target. However, the Department will not be in a position to measure progress towards the 90 per cent target until the Government Procurement Card has been rolled out to the whole Department and until full functionality has been rolled out on the Department's ORACLE-based Resource Accounting and Budgeting system. We intend to start formal monitoring in Spring 2000.

Import and export procedures completed electronically: There are a number of ongoing initiatives within HM Customs and Excise aimed at simplification and computerisation of customs procedures:

— Customs Freight Simplified Procedures (CFSP) were introduced in 1998 and, in many cases, removed the need for a customs declaration and supporting documentation to be submitted in paper at the frontier. Authorised traders are instead allowed to supply full details of the goods to Customs, at a later date, by means of Electronic Data Interchange (EDI) and retain supporting documents at their premises to be checked on an audit basis. Phase II of the project was completed on 31 March 1999. It has increased the scope of the system by allowing both Excise goods and further CAP goods to be imported under CFSP. As of 23 April 1999, there are 36 traders operating CFSP and 103 applications are being processed.

— Building on the messaging systems developed for CFSP, Customs are also participating in an EU wide Single European Authorisation (SEA) project to facilitate multi-national traders. This will allow the trader to appoint a single centre of administration within the EU for the operation of their simplified import and export procedures. This project is currently in its pilot phase.

— UK Customs area also working in partnership with US Customs and multi-national companies to develop prototype systems to reduce procedural barriers to international trade, standardise customs procedures and enhance mutual assistance between customs services. The International Trade Prototype (ITP) project will make use of both secure Internet services and EDIFACT messaging for the exchange of data. A seamless transaction will be created with the electronic export declaration becoming the import declaration in the importing country. The first prototype will be introduced in 1999.

— UK Customs are working with counterparts of G7 countries to standardise electronic customs declarations across G7 countries, reflecting the global nature of international trade. Work on the EDIFACT message is proceeding in tandem with the work on the import and export data sets and a prototype will be developed to test both sets.

— In response to fraud within the Community/Common Transit system, Customs aim to implement in the UK a computerised transit system, being developed by the EU, to control transit movements. The system will meet specific UK requirements as well as the EU requirement. It will be implemented sometime between 2000 and 2002.

— As well as the work already carried out on simplified procedures, Customs are looking at extending the use of paperless systems to normal import procedures. There area a number of legal and procedural issues which need to be resolved before this can be accomplished. One of the main areas to be addressed concerns the acceptance of electronic authentication for customs declarations. Work is being undertaken by Custom's Information Systems Directorate in conjunction with Trade Policy Group to develop a solution for electronic customs declarations.

Another area concerns the treatment of supporting documentation to enable traders to retain documents outside the scope of simplified procedures requires an amendment to EU legislation. Negotiations are ongoing to resolve this matter in the European Council's Economic Questions Group UK Customs are participating in these negotiations.

— Customs are also developing an electronic system for the control and processing of export declarations which will facilitate the move to an inland system of audit based control. This will allow for the presentation of minimal pre-shipment data with the certainty of fast track frontier clearance. A number of options have been developed to cater for different types of exporters and work on the implementation of these options is ongoing.

Within the DTI, the Export Control Organisation (ECO) introduced a new licence application form on 1 March 1999. The form can be completed electronically and submitted to ECO on floppy disk. The system is called ELATE. Although supporting documents, such as End User details and technical specifications, still need to be provided on paper, there are significant advantages for the exporter as license details can be quickly copied from one application to the next. The need for re-keying details of paper applications when they are received by ECO has been eliminated, reducing transcription errors and speeding-up the process. The system also allows application details to be transmitted electronically to MoD and FCO, removing a further stage of data input and delay. It is expected that electronic transmission will be expanded to include all advisory departments in the near future.

The ELATE system is the first step in providing a fully electronic application system for export licenses. It will be followed by an application allowing End User details and technical specifications to be sent electronically. Some obstacles, such as data security and digital signature verification, limit the introduction of a fully electronic system and are currently being considered. Introduction of the Government Secure Intranet to all advisory departments is also a prerequisite to secure transmission. It is envisaged that all these functions will be available by 2002. The final link in the chain will be the issue of electronic licenses to the exporter and Customs and Excise. Discussions are underway, but a system of this type is dependent on the availability of the full set of electronic applications described above.

9. *The Committee would be grateful for some further details about the legislation announced to let firms file VAT and PAYE returns electronically, including the nature of the discount to be offered on electronic returns; and more information on the "Internet based self service facility" to be launched by the Inland Revenue and HM Customs and Excise (Inland Revenue, Press Notice, 9 March 1999)*

Legislation for Electronic Returns: The legislation announced in the Budget to allow firms to file VAT and tax returns electronically is to be found in Clauses 123 and 124 of Finance Bill 1999. The Clauses give taxpayers and tax authorities the option to use electronic communication even where there is an existing statutory requirement to communicate in writing. The Clauses do not aim to set out in detail the ways in which taxpayers and tax authorities can communicate electronically. Instead they provide powers for regulations which could govern two-way electronic communication between taxpayers and tax authorities and electronic payment to tax authorities.

Clauses also contain powers to set out conditions which must be met if electronic communication is to have the same legal effect as communication by writing on paper. This will allow departments to ensure that for example all the statutory obligations in respect of returns apply to all taxpayers irrespective of whether they choose to make a written return on paper or send the information electronically. The Clause also allows for provisions in respect of the use of intermediaries for example Internet service providers and certifying authorities so that the conditions for electronic communication can be adapted to meet changing conditions. Overall the Clauses provide the framework for more detailed secondary legislation which will be able to encompass all forms of electronic communication between taxpayers and tax authorities.

Discounts: The legislation in question does not deal with discounts for electronic returns referred to in the Budget. The proposal to offer a discount on returns filed via the Internet is part of the package of increased support for small businesses which the Chancellor announced in the Budget. The level of the discount, which returns it will apply to and when it will be introduced are all matters the government is currently considering.

Internet Based Self Service Facility: This will take the form of a pilot system to be built around the circumstances of an individual (the customer) wishing to open up a new business employing staff. It will seek to demonstrate that it is possible to provide in one place and in a useable way the range of services and information that the customer needs to comply with regulations on opening a business and employing staff. The pilot system will steer the customer through the actions to be taken, the legislation to be observed and the support available from the government. It will also seek to reduce the number of "hand offs" from one point of government to another that might typically be encountered at present. It will provide links to other sources of information that might be useful in the process of setting up a successful new business.

The pilot is being funded through HM Treasury's Invest to Save Budget. The Inland Revenue is taking the lead, with DTI, HM Customs and Excise, Health and Safety Executive, DfEE, Employment Service, and Norwich City Council as partners.

TELECOMMINICATIONS COSTS

10. *It would be helpful to know a little more about the DTI's approach to the European Commission on the price of leased lines in the EU relative to the US, the response received, and an indication of future action to be taken by DTI on this issue. (Memorandum, paragraph 4.8)*

The DTI has raised the issue of cost of leased lines in Europe with the European Commission in a number of fora, including the Open Network Provision Committee (set up under the EU ONP Directives including the Leased Lines Directive 97/51/EC) and the High Level Committee of Telecoms Regulators. The Commission has recently sought updated information on leased line prices from all Member States in order to assess whether national telecoms regulators are correctly enforcing the provisions of the Leased Lines Directive. The UK has encouraged the Commission to carry out this examination speedily.

The price of leased lines is also being considered by the Commision as part of the current review of EU telecoms liberalisation legislation which is due to conclude by the end of 1999. When we receive the Commission's findings we will want to look at them closely with a view to considering whether there is a need for any strengthening of the provisions of the Leased Lines Directive.

CONSUMER CREDIT ACT 1974

11. *Could you inform the Committee of what plans DTI has to extend section 75 of the Consumer Credit Act 1974 to cover overseas transactions, and when such plans are likely to be implemented (Qq226, 287–88)?*

The impact of section 75 on overseas transactions is unclear and has not been clarified by the courts. We have no evidence that UK consumers are suffering any detriment at present and we have no plans to make any changes to the legislation.

UNIVERSITY FOR INDUSTRY

12. *It would be helpful for the Committee to be updated on the current status of the University for Industry and its relationship with DTI's electronic commerce agenda*

University for Industry—The UfI will be a new kind of organisation for open and distance learning aimed at both individuals and businesses. Using modern ICTs, it will broker high quality learning products and services and make them available at home, in the workplace and at learning centres country-wide. It will have two strategic objectives:

— to stimulate demand for lifelong learning amongst businesses and individuals

— to promote the availability of, and improve access to, relevant, high quality and innovative learning opportunities through the use of ICTs

UfI services will be launched nationally in Autumn 2000.

An external transition advisory board, chaired by Lord David Sainsbury, and a transition team were established in May 1998 to develop legal and administrative structures and initial business plans for UfI. A draft three year corporate plan was subsequently submitted to DfEE Ministers in December 1998, and was accepted as a basis for future planning and for negotiating contractual arrangements with the DfEE.

Responsibility for taking forward the plans now rests with UfI Ltd and its permanent board.

A press conference on 18 March 1999 launched UfI Ltd's development plans, its public statement of plans leading to national launch in Autumn 2000. Over the next two years a number of development projects will test out aspects of the UfI model. A call for bids was made under the EU's ADAPT programme. Around 118 projects have been accepted. Projects started in September 1998. Early lessons from these will be drawn out and fed in to the UfI's development process.

Also on 18 March, an extra £4 million funding for UfI in 1999–2000 was announced, in addition to the £40 million already announced, to provide a firm foundation for the UfI to take forward its development and implementation plans towards the launch.

Learning Direct, the national learning information helpline, was launched on 25 February. The helpline has been a resounding success, helping over 513,000 callers with free, high quality information and advice. Learning Direct will become the UfI's information service while continuing to offer a comprehensive, impartial helpline. £6.25 million has been allocated in 1999–2000, to enable Learning Direct to develop its services to cope with the extra demand for learning created by the UfI.

*UfI and DTI's e-commerce agenda:* The UfI will promote the availability of, and improve access to, relevant high quality and innovative learning, particularly through the use of ICTs. Increasing IT skill levels through the expansion of learning opportunities is one of UfI's initial priorities. The development of e-commerce systems will be an important area for UfI to take into account in developing relevant and up to date learning materials, as well as consideration for the organisation itself of how it runs its own business.

*19 May 1999*

## APPENDIX 2

**Supplementary memorandum submitted by the Department of Trade and Industry**

Moving into the Information Age: International/Regional/Sectoral Benchmarking Studies 1999

I am enclosing copies of three reports, *Moving into the Information Age—International/Regional/Sectoral Benchmarking Studies 1999.*[1] These studies were undertaken as part of DTI's Information Society Initiative (ISI). I am sure you will find them relevant to your enquiry into e-commerce, not least because they track the progress of UK business towards the "one million wired-up SMEs' target in the Competitiveness White Paper, which we discussed when I gave evidence to the Committee in March.

The studies are based on the latest wave of primary research tracking levels of ownership, use and understanding of information and communication technologies (ICTs) by businesses in seven countries: UK, US, Japan, Germany, France, Italy and Canada. These reports are the latest in a series of benchmarking studies undertaken as part of the ISI. The research assesses the development of the seven countries over the past year, compares attitudes and levels of awareness and analyses drivers and barriers to change. It also draws on a series of interviews with UK SMEs to gain a better understanding of the issues affecting smaller firms. An overview of the aims, results and conclusions is presented in the first chapter of the International report. Also, for the first time, a complete regional breakdown of the results has been presented, as well as a breakdown of results for eight sectors selected to represent a cross-section of UK industry (Chemicals, Defence and Aerospace, Retail (not food and drink), Road Haulage, Insurance Services, Advertising, Clothing and Vehicle Components).

Three key points emerge from the International report:

— there has been rapid development is most areas of uptake and use of ICTs, in particular in networked technologies. The UK has largely caught up with the main G7 leaders in the US, although many of the UK's smallest businesses are clearly some way behind, (however the UK's position as European leader is very much under threat with very rapid growth in Germany bringing them up to the UK's overall position);

— the UK is on course to meet its target of "one million SMEs wired up to the digital marketplace by 2002" up to two years early, with 600,000 now connected, compared to just 350,000 last year. Stephen Byers is therefore extending our original target to 1.5 million connected SMEs, and introducing a new target of one million SMEs actually trading (ie purchasing or selling) on line, by 2002;

— Despite the very strong overall growth, the report also demonstrates a much greater disparity of performance within the UK's economy than in any other benchmarked country, with our larger firms (> 100 employees) amongst the best for their size bands, but with our small firms (10–99 employees) below the G7 average and our micro firms (< 10 employees) the poorest of any benchmarked country. Accordingly, Stephen Byers is also setting a third target, to bring the ICT performance of our smaller firms up to the level of the best in the G7.

Four key points emerge from the Regional report:

— London is very much out on its own, leading the UK into the Information Age, and leaving other regions in its wake;

— the figures for London, due to the very high levels of employment there, greatly influence the UK's total average figure. Business in the West Midlands, the South East, the North West and the Eastern Regions are performing on or around the UK average. However, the remaining regions of the UK fall well below average, and are thus also performing significantly behind their main competitors in the G7;

— Wales and Northern Ireland, due to their very long tail of smaller businesses have performed particularly badly, and are clearly a step behind the rest of the country;

— business use of Government initiatives and support organisations for access to information about ICTs is high across the whole of the UK and is the highest of the G7 countries. Furthermore, of those who use them, well over a third made successful changes to their businesses as a result, and over half felt that the staff were knowledgeable and the advice relevant for their businesses. This demonstrates the importance that businesses in the UK place on the services supplied by the Government through the Business Links and other organisations.

Two key messages emerged from the Sectoral report:

— knowledge intensive industry sectors such as Advertising and Chemicals are more advanced users of ICTs across the range of business functions, while businesses in the more traditional sectors such as retailing and clothing manufacturing are less connected and less interested in using these technologies in any aspect of their processes;

---

[1] Not printed.

— the sectors that have performed better than expected can attribute their success to the influence of large companies championing change through the supply chain.

*25 May 1999*

# APPENDIX 3

## Memorandum submitted by Mr Thomas Long, Atlantic Fellow in Public Policy, University of Glasgow School of Law

INTRODUCTION AND SUMMARY

I am submitting this memorandum as a supplement to the statement I wrote for the Campaign for Unmetered Telecommunications (CUT) and which CUT attached to its April 1999 submission to this Committee. In particular, I wish to respond specifically to statements and suggestions regarding unmetered local calling in the US appearing in Oftel's March 1999 memorandum.

This memo makes the following points:

— Unmetered calling is enormously popular in the US.

— Unmetered calling promotes civic affairs, universal service, local commerce, and E-commerce.

— Unmetered calling is consistent with excellent service quality and has had no adverse effect on the ability to connect calls in the US.

— Unmetered calling does not undermine investment incentives or capabilities.

— Unmetered calling in the US is not dependent on cross subsidies from other services.

— Unmetered calling is not responsible for the lack of residential local competition thus far in the US.

— The absence of unmetered calling in the UK is the result of market failure, the remedy for which requires regulatory intervention.

STATEMENT OF QUALIFICATIONS

I have been an advocate for the interests of residential and small business telecoms users in California for almost a decade. My organisation, TURN, is a nonprofit consumer advocacy organisation that specialises in telecoms, electricity, and gas issues. We are completely independent of government and receive most of our funding from membership contributions and from attorneys' fees in matters in which we are found to have made substantial contribution. Though TURN is independent of government, we have a right of access to all of the information on which the regulators rely in reaching their decisions. Through my access to such information, I have a detailed understanding of the economics of the telecoms industry in the US.

In recognition of my achievements and leadership position in my field, I have been awarded an Atlantic Fellowship in Public Policy. The fellowship is sponsored and funded by the UK and enables Americans to conduct research about UK-based developments in their fields. Since September 1998, I have been researching telecoms regulation in the UK, examining in particular the UK's efforts to promote local (access) competition. Although I am far from an expert regarding UK telecoms regulation, my nine months of research here (including several dozen interviews with key players in the industry) perhaps make me uniquely qualified to make comparisons and draw informed conclusions regarding key telecoms issues in our two nations.

THE ENORMOUS POPULARITY OF UNMETERED CALLING IN THE US

Before specifically addressing Oftel's memorandum, some context regarding unmetered calling in the US is necessary. When establishing telephone service, most[2] residential customers in the US have a choice between flat and measured local service. Flat service means that, for a fixed monthly charge, the customer may make an unlimited number of local calls of unlimited duration at any time of day or night, all without any additional charge. This is fully unmetered local calling. Measured service carries a substantially lower monthly charge than flat service (the differential is often $5 or more), but requires the customer to pay for most local calls on a usage basis. Even measured service is not always fully metered; some measured service offerings, as in California, include an allowance of uncharged local calls. Nevertheless, measured service is the closest the US has to BT's scheme of charging for the "line rental" and for all local calls on a usage basis.

Flat service is enormously popular in the US. Despite its relatively high price compared to measured service, the vast majority of California residents (over 85 per cent) take flat service.

---

[2] I say "most" because local rates are a matter for state regulation and each state has a separate scheme of local rate regulation. Still, there is broad similarity among the various state schemes.

THE BENEFITS OF UNMETERED CALLING

There are several reasons for the popularity of flat service in the US. *First, it promotes civic affairs.* Citizens can call their neighbours regarding community, school, and church meetings and activities without extra charge. Likewise, charitable or political organisations can raise money or engage in get-out-the-vote efforts without extra charge.

*Second, it promotes local commerce.* Unmetered calling enables US consumers to do a considerable amount of shopping by telephone, especially to determine in advance whether a particular merchant has a product meeting the customer's specifications (eg, shoes in the right style and size). This makes shopping more convenient and benefits the environment by curtailing unnecessary uses of the car (upon which Americans are far too reliant). A 1998 McKinsey report found that, on a per capita basis, for every 100 call minutes in the US, there are only 37 in the UK[3]. The report found "considerable evidence" that "many of the calls foregone in the UK are . . . consumer-to-business calls . . . , calls that might have created economic value"[4]

Third, it promotes universal service. Consumers have the security of knowing exactly how much they will be billed for local service at the end of the month, which greatly assists in keeping people connected to the telephone network.

Fourth, and perhaps most relevant to this Committee, flat service promotes Internet use and E-commerce. Internet searches do not lend themselves to time constraints, as one piece of information typically leads to another path of research that may have been previously unforeseen. If consumers cannot afford to stay on-line to complete their desired research or browsing, they are not able to exploit the Internet's full potential. Moreover, many software applications assume that the consumer has an open link to the Internet. However, with metered calling, keeping the link open is cost prohibitive, again preventing many consumers from taking full advantage of their computer.

The detrimental impact on E-commerce is evident. If consumers cannot afford to browse, they are less likely to use the Internet for shopping. Many businesses that have a strong marketing base in the UK do not have sufficient UK demand for Internet shopping to sustain E-commerce operations. internet shopping is now dominated by Americans and, hence, American corporations. UK businesses may be missing a time-limited opportunity to establish a presence in the world of E-commerce.

In light of the enormous benefits to consumers and the economy from unmetered local service, it is right for this Committee to ask why most UK consumers have no meaningful choice of unmetered service.

RESPONSE TO OFTEL MEMORANDUM

Oftel suggests that unmetered calling in the US has resulted in problems of four different types. I wish to respond to each of the supposed problems.

Capacity overload. Oftel suggests in paragraphs 32 and 33 that unmetered local calls make it likely that network capacity will be overwhelmed. Oftel even claims that, in the US, "it has been known, in some instances, for calls to emergency services to not get through."

I can assure you that a capacity overload that prevented the completion of a call to emergency services would be treated with the utmost seriousness by any telecoms regulator in the US. I am aware of no such instance since the explosion in Internet use. In California, the state with the highest concentration of Internet users, there is absolutely no problem completing calls of any type as any time of day or night.

Effects on investment. Oftel claims (paragraph 34) that unmetered calling creates the need for additional investment to increase network capacity, but that the lack of additional revenue from increased call minutes prevents local operators from recovering the cost of that additional investment.

Oftel fails to consider, however, that additional local calling stimulates demand for additional phone lines, which significantly enhances the revenues of local operators. When a household phone line is tied up with an Internet connection for long periods, the household often decides to add one or more lines. Additional lines is an area of fast growth for US local operators.

With respect to advanced infrastructure investment, Pacific Bell, the largest incumbent local operator in California, is well ahead of BT in terms of offering broadband DSL service over copper phone lines. Moreover, Pacific Bell earns healthy profits for its parent SBC Communications, one of the largest and most financially secure phone companies in the US.

*Cross-subsidy.* Oftel suggests in paragraphs 30 and 31 that consumers in the US are paying for unmetered calling either through very high monthly fixed charges or through inflated charges for non-local calling.

The additional monthly charges for flat service are not so high as to make the service undesirable. As noted previously, consumers have a choice between metered and unmetered calling and they willingly pay $5 or more extra per month in order to enjoy unmetered calling. In my statement attached to the CUT submission, I showed that, in California, the monthly charges for flat service are only £2.50 per month higher than BT's

---

[3]McKinsey Global Institute, *Driving Productivity and Growth in the UK Economy,* October 1998, p15 (hereinafter "McKinsey Report").

[4]McKinsey Report, p17.

line rental. For that additional amount, customers can make all the local calls they desire, which would carry a high price tag in the UK. (Unfortunately, I lack data regarding the volume and time-of-day distrubution of local calling in the US that would allow me to quantify the price for a typical basket of US local calling at BT's rates.)

In my CUT statement, I also explained that it is incorrect to view local rates in the US as receiving a subsidy from long distance rates.

Additional rate comparisons I have made since I prepared my statement for CUT also suggest that charges for local calling in the US are dramatically lower than in the UK and that long distance rates in the US do not offset this large differential[5].

My results are summarised in the following tables:

### Comparison of Residential Local Rates in the US (California) and UK

|  | *US* | *UK* | *% Difference* |
| --- | --- | --- | --- |
| *Line Rental*[6] *( $/month)* | $10.78 | $12.14 | +13% |
| *Local usage (5 min call in cents)* |  |  |  |
| Day | 6.6 | 27.0 | +309% |
| Evening | 4.6 | 10.0 | +117% |
| Weekend | 2.9 | 6.8 | +134% |

Source: US—Pacific Bell rates, UK—BT rates

### Comparison of Residential Long Distance Rates of Local Operators in the US (California) and the UK
### (charges for a five minute call in cents)

|  | *US (21–40 miles)* | *UK* | *% Difference* |
| --- | --- | --- | --- |
| Day | 42.0 | 54.0 | +29% |
| Evening | 33.6 | 28.5 | −15% |
| Weekend | 25.2 | 20.0 | −21% |

Source: US—Pacific Bell rates, UK—BT rates

The first table is the closest possible approximation of a like-to-like comparison of local rates given the absence of unmetered calling in the UK. Monthly line rental charges are at least 13 per cent higher in the UK than in California. UK local usage charges are more than double those in the US, and in the daytime period, UK charges are over four times higher.

The second table examines the most comparable non-local rates in California and the UK. The US rates shown are for intrastate regional long distance calls (called intraLATA calls in US jargon) provided by Pacific Bell.[7] In the daytime period, the UK rates are higher, whereas in the evening and weekend periods, the UK rates are lower.

Thus, even with most of its residential customers taking unmetered local service, Pacific Bell is able to offer a substantially better deal for local service than BT, while offering a broadly comparable deal for long distance calls.

Effect on local competition. Oftel suggests (paragraph 35) that unmetered local calling in the US has stifled local competition. In particular, Oftel notes that UK cable operators offer telecoms competition for more than half of BT's residential lines, while in the US there is minimal local competition.

Oftel is correct that there is considerably more local competition here than in the US, but draws improper inferences from the difference. There are several reasons for the absence of residential local competition in the US, none of them related to unmetered local calling. First, the US only fully opened its local markets to

---

[5] I acknowledge that, because of geographic and market structure differences in our two countries, such comparisons are complex and require difficult exercises of judgment. Unfortunately, I have not been able to examine the Eurodata comparisons cited by Oftel because that research is proprietary and only available by subscription.

[6] As a US surrogate for the UK line rental, I have used the monthly charge for measured service, which in California, also includes five uncharged directory enquiries plus an allowance of unmetered calls worth an additional $3.00/month. Thus, the percentage difference shown understates the extent to which line rentals in the UK are more expensive than in the US.

[7] Unlike those of BT, Pacific Bell's rates vary by distance. I have used the distance range in which the highest number of regional long distance calls fall. For shorter distances, Pacific Bell's rates are lower than those shown in the table, and for longer distances, the rates are higher.

competition in 1996, five years after the UK ended its duopoly policy. As the US well knows, it takes several years to implement the complex regulatory framework for local competition. Second, federalism problems have significantly delayed the construction of that framework in the US. Third, cable operators in the US deployed their television networks in the 1960s and 1970s, long before they contempleted providing telephone service. In contrast, the UK cable operators (with a high level of US ownership) had the advantage of a much later start and being able to design their networks to include copper wire for telephony.

### Conclusion

The US experience and the concerted efforts of groups like CUT show that consumers want unmetered calling. If there were a truly competitive market for local telephone service, operators would surely strive to meet this demand by offering attractive unmetered local calling options. The US experience shows that it is possible to offer fully unmetered local calling, while providing first-class telecoms service and excellent value for money, and sustaining a financially healthy telecoms industry.

The competition that BT faces, almost entirely from the cable operators, is not strong enough to force BT to satisfy customer demand for unmetered service. The absence of unmetered calling in the UK is the result of the failure of limited and imperfect competition to deliver what consumers want. To remedy such market failure, regulatory intervention is necessary.

*20 May 1999*

## APPENDIX 4

### Memorandum submitted by the Vodafone Group

### Introduction

1. The Vodafone Group (Vodafone) was awarded one of the original two UK cellular mobile communications licences in 1982. Today Vodafone is a leading global provider of mobile telecommunications services, owning interests in mobile operations in 13 countries in Europe, Africa and Australia. In the UK Vodafone has maintained its market leadership position since 1986, and currently it has over six million customers to whom it offers voice, data, information and early mobile e-commerce services.

2. The Vodafone Group announced in January this year that it is to merge with AirTouch Communications Inc, an international mobile business based in the US. The merger will create Europe's most valuable telecommunications group and the world's largest, and first truly global, mobile phone company. The Group will have a market capitalisation of around £70 billion, operations in 24 countries and over 27 million customers. This will make it the second or third largest company in the UK. (For more details see Annex 4).

3. Vodafone believes that mobile phones can provide a substantial part of the infrastructure for e-commerce, especially for consumers and SMEs. This is because mobile communications networks provide a universal, convenient, personalised and secure technology, features that are clearly important for e-commerce. Vodafone intends to promote mobile e-commerce as a natural way for people to transact much of their day-to-day business. It intends to lead the way in mobile e-commerce, and by doing so help fulfil the Prime Minister's stated desire to see Britain lead the world in electronic commerce.

4. Whilst a number of mobile e-commerce services are already being offered (and others are under development) they all tend to suffer from not being particularly easy to use, especially for those who are not technically minded. Over the next few years, however, several technology developments are going to reach the market that will make e-commerce much more accessible. The first of these developments is GPRS (General Packet Radio System), which allows fast packet data communications over the GSM mobile system. This will considerably improve data transaction rates. A second development is WAP (Wireless Application Protocol), which will provide for web browsing capability in the mobile phone. A third is SAT (SIM application toolkit), which will provide for transaction security to banking standards. Taken together, these developments will allow more, and more user friendly, e-commerce services to be offered on the mobile phone.

5. We therefore regard it as critical, that the mobile communications dimension is included in the continuing debate on e-commerce issues, and that the mobile industry makes sure that it contributes positively to the debate.

### What are the Benefits of Mobile E-commerce?

6. Mobile e-commerce means simply conducting secure transactions, not necessarily involving payment, through the use of mobile phones. The Global Mobile Commerce Forum (GMCF), a forum for parties interested in developing mobile e-commerce, defines mobile e-commerce as "the delivery of electronic commerce capabilities directly into the consumer's hand via wireless technology". Examples of mobile e-commerce are electronic ticketing, opinion polling, access to secured environments and, of course, the purchase of goods and services. (More examples are given in Annexes 2 and 3).

7. The compelling characteristics of the mobile phone as an enabler of e-commerce are that it is personal, convenient, its technology is secure and ever advancing and it will soon be used universally. The potential for the mobile phone as a core technology for conducting e-commerce has not, in Vodafone's opinion, been given sufficient attention in the e-commerce debate. Consequently the benefits that it could bring have not been adequately explored or discussed. In our view, the benefits of mobile e-commerce are that it is:

Personal: Unlike the PC or TV, that tend to be household items for family use, the mobile phone is personal equipment usually belonging to an individual, and being used to deliver a personal service to that individual.

Convenient: Mobile phones are networked electronic devices which people carry around so that they can be on-line whenever and wherever they wish.

Secure: Mobile phones used on a GSM digital network contain a programmable smart card, called a SIM (subscriber identity modules). This device contains all the data needed by a customer to gain access to a network, and is both secure and reliable. It has the potential to be used to provide all the security features and functions that are going to be so essential for widespread adpotion of electronic commerce. In this respect the mobile phone industry has much to contribute to the uptake of e-commerce, both in terms of technology and in the management of smart cards issued to a large customer base.

Advanced: Mobile phone technology is advanced and continues to improve. Customers are used to changing their mobile phones so as to benefit from new services, features and designs as they are introduced. Today people change their mobile phones on average every three years (whereas the replacement cycle of the fixed phone and TV is several times longer), and there is every indication that this trend will continue. Mobile phones therefore provide an excellent vehicle for introducing the new technology required for e-commerce.

Universal: Today over 15 million people, more than a quarter of the UK population and around a third of those aged 16 and over, have a mobile phone, and they tend to carry it with them everywhere. In less than five years, the financial community forecasts that the number of mobile phones in use in the UK will be over half the total population and roughly the equivalent of one per working adult (see Annex 1.) Therefore the provision of e-commerce capability in the mobile phone promises to make e-commerce available to half the population of the country.

## ELECTRONIC PAYMENT SYSTEMS

8. Mobile phones are a ready-made vehicle for electronic payment systems. The modern mobile phone was designed to include advanced crytographic security features for authenticating users and protecting user traffic from eavesdropping on the radio link. Future generations of phones will include security features that make it a secure means of payment via credit, debit or electronic cash cards for Internet purchases or pay-per-view TV.

## ELECTRONIC GOVERNMENT

9. Vodaphone understands that the Government is trying to bring about a fundamental change to the way in which it conducts its business. As well as trying to achieve better co-ordination between different governmental departments, it is looking for ways in which it can provide "new, efficient and convenient ways for citizens and businesses to communicate with government and receive services."

The Government has set itself the target of being able to conduct 25 per cent of its business electronically by 2002, 50 per cent by 2005 and 100 per cent by 2008. Vodafone agrees that the Government's strategy for achieving these goals needs to be flexible to reflect technological developments and is pleased to contribute to the debate by being part of the Government's Information Age Partnership.

This is because Vodafone believes that the Government's targets cannot be viewed in isolation from the rest of the UK. For Britain to lead the world in electronic commerce, it does have to be a joint industry and Government initiative.

10. Having said that, Vodafone believes that the mobile networks may have a significant role to play in the specific provision of electronic government. They could, for example, facilitate the emergence of electronic voting, through the secure communications afforded by personal mobile phones. People would no longer have to attend a polling station to vote, and this alone might help to foster greater participation in elections. Whether at home or abroad, people would be able to download voting forms to their phone and vote on issues of personal or national or European interest.

11. Digital signature technology is going to be extremely important for both electronic commerce, and electronic Government, especially where electronic payment or legally binding authorisation is required. Since mobile phones are portable and personal communication terminals, they offer huge potential as hosts for digital signature mechanisms. What could be more convenient than to sign a person electronic cheque or electronic income tax return using one's mobile phone? To realise this we must ensure that it is feasible to generate and transmit legally recognised digital signatures within the contraints of mobile technology. This is another reason why it is important that the mobile communications sector contributes to the electronic commerce debate.

### THE VISION OF MOBILE E-COMMERCE

12. The demand for mobile e-commerce will grow as consumers have a choice in the way they access information and conduct transactions. They will need to be able to do so when, where and how they find it most convenient and useful. This includes when they are travelling internationally, whether on business or holiday. With the current European GSM network standard, and with the proposed world-wide third generation standard (UMTS), people will be able to make mobile e-commerce transactions wherever they are. They will use the same familiar terminal, the same language, and with the same ease of use as when they are at home in the UK.

13. In time, any transaction that can be made in the wired environment will be possible via a mobile phone either directly from a mobile terminal, or with an attachment such as a portable PC. Moreover, the mobile phone will provide the added benefit of being personal and with one at all times. Mobile phone networks will therefore play a parallel and complementary role to the fixed Internet. They will offer both a wireless connection to the Internet, and direct access to providers of goods and services that are specifically tailored to meet the needs of people whilst they are on the move.

14. Furthermore, as mobile phones are personal, an important focus of the industry is the customisation of services for consumers—something that is not always offered by fixed carriers or Internet service providers. Customisation enables consumers to tailor the services they receive to reflect their own interests and requirements, and ensures that they only receive the informaiton and promotions they have requrested on subjects of their own choice.

15. For example, customers could create their own tailored news service delivered by either e-mail or a short message to their mobile phone. Vodafone believes that, like in ordinary commerce, effective customisation will have an important role to play in the promotion of e-commerce.

16. Vodafone agrees with the Government that all members of society should have access to e-commerce. It is committed to helping to achieve this by leading the way in providing customised, easy-to-use and secure e-commerce services to the rapidly expanding number of digital mobile phone users. It will encourage uptake by tailoring its service and payment packages to different sectors of the population. We are convinced that if e-commerce is to flourish, there is just as much a need to understand the requirements for sectorisation in that business as there is in mobile communications. The mobile industry experienced considerable growth with the introduction of prepayment as a way of appealing to people who did not wish to pay subscription charges.

### UK LEADERSHIP IN MOBILE E-COMMERCE

17. The natural vehicle for e-commerce has to date been the Internet, a technology which is essentially from the US. One of the problems with the Internet is security, a problem that will constrain e-commerce if it is not solved.

18. To properly address the security problem requires new technology, like smart cards with digital signature applications, in the hands of users, enabling them to access the Internet and securely. Consumer priced PCs do not provide this technology, and there is little indication that they will do so in the near future. In contrast, mobile phones already provide this technology, albeit in the embryonic form of the GSM SIM. With the next generation of mobile phones, from 2002 onwards, we can expect a complete set of security functions designed specifically to support e-commerce. This is technically achievable. All that is required is for the mobile phone industry to make it happen, and Vodafone will commit its expertise in this area to help do just that.

19. The UK and Europe are world leaders in mobile communications, and this leadership provides opportunities for the UK and Europe to shape the agenda for the future of the industry. The UK, in particular, has the opportunity to capitalise on this advantage by developing a world lead in mobile e-commerce. The UK led Europe in the introduction of cellular technology, and Europe has been a leader in developing mobile communications standards that have been adopted throughout much of the world. In contrast, the US lags considerably behind Europe in the services that are offered by its mobile communications operators, including mobile data services. This is due in part to the fragmentation of its

mobile industry, and in part to a lack of national licensing and common standards. This recognition of the benefits of standardisation could be extremely important in ensuring Europe takes the lead in mobile e-commerce. The influence of the UK mobile community, and Vodafone in particular, on the European standards making bodies could play a significant part in making the UK a leader in mobile e-commerce.

20. Furthermore, with its proposed merger with AirTouch, Vodafone will be in a strong position to help the UK to take a worldwide lead in mobile e-commerce. Combining Vodafone's position in mobile with AirTouch's position as a major US company provides the opportunity to promote e-commerce across the globe through mobile access to the Internet.

21. This is an important opportunity as telecommunications is one of the UK's top three industries and one of the world's fastest growing sectors.

An Infrastructure for Social Inclusion

22. The booming demand for mobile communications provides an opportunity for everyone to participate in the e-commerce revolution. Mobile phones are popular and, with new ways of paying for the service attracting whole new sectors of customers, soon most of the population will have one. In the UK over 25 per cent of the population have a mobile phone and, with innovations like prepayment, the number is growing by over 500,000 per month. In Finland the penetration has reached almost 60 per cent of the population, and the UK is expected to follow.

23. To put these statistics into perspective, it is estimated that there are far more mobile phones in the UK than there are PCs in homes, and Vodafone believe there are more than twice as many mobile phones in the UK than home Internet connections. (A BMRB survey for The Henley Centre estimates a figure of 21 per cent of households in the UK have Internet connection. This gives a figure of approximately 5 million compared with more than 14 million mobile phones.)

24. The profile of a typical mobile phone user is also changing and widening. It is no longer the wealthy businessman. In recent years the costs of owing a cellular phone have dropped dramatically, and the introduction of prepayment tariffs, giving customers control over their expenditure, has enabled people from all walks of life—young and old, male and female, worker and student—to use mobile phones. Prepayment tariffs appear to appeal particularly to the young, those on lower incomes and those without the use of a fixed phone. The upfront cost of a mobile phone on a prepayment tariff today is £70 (inclusive of some talk time). The barriers to entry for people to make and receive mobile calls, and in future to make mobile e-commerce transactions, are low and reducing all the time. The result is a widening appeal to an increasing proportion of population.

The mobile phone has the potential to take e-commerce proactively to consumers, including those who might once have never thought that they would become users of e-commerce.

*Summary*

Mobile phones will provide the consumer and the business user with an infrastructure for e-commerce. The network infrastructure already exists and soon everyone, from all walks of life, will be carrying around their personal networked e-commerce handset.

Vodafone, as the UK market leader in mobile communications, will help to create this vision through active and intense promotion of e-commerce using mobile phones, and by development of the technology needed to provide it. Vodafone hopes that this will help the Government achieve its targets for widespread adoption of e-commerce by all sectors of our community and its more specific targets for Government.

*24 June 1999*

**Annex 1**

MARKET FORECASTS

FORECAST OF UK MOBILE PHONE CUSTOMERS (MILLIONS)

| Forecaster | Date of Forecast | 31–3–99 Actual | 31–3–00 | 31–3–02 | 31–3–04 |
|---|---|---|---|---|---|
| Bear Stearns | Mar 99 | 14.9 | 19.9 | 26.4 | 31.6 |
| Salomon Smith Barney | Mar 99 | 14.9 | 20.3 | 28.2 | n/a |
| J P Morgan | Apr 99 | 14.9 | 20.5 | 29.7 | n/a |
| Warburg Dillon Read | Mar 99 | 14.9 | 20.7 | 32.7 | 39.1 |

FORECAST OF UK MOBILE PHONE PENETRATION OF POPULATION (BASED ON 59.0 MILLION POPULATION)

| Forecaster | Date of Forecast | 31–3–99 Actual | 31–3–00 | 31–3–02 | 31–3–04 |
|---|---|---|---|---|---|
| Bear Stearns | Mar 99 | 25.2% | 33.7% | 44.8% | 53.6% |
| Salomon Smith Barney | Mar 99 | 25.2% | 34.3% | 47.7% | n/a |
| JP Morgan | Apr 99 | 25.2% | 34.8% | 50.3% | n/a |
| Warburg Dillon Read | Mar 99 | 25.2% | 35.1% | 55.4% | 66.3% |

UK POPULATION STATISTICS FOR MID-1997 IN MILLIONS (SOURCE: ONS)

| Total Resident Population | Adults of Working Age (16 to 64/59) | All Adults (16+) |
|---|---|---|
| 59.0 | 36.2 | 46.9 |

**Annex 2**

## EXAMPLES OF MOBILE E-COMMERCE

### ELECTRONIC TICKETS

25. People will be able to search a train timetable, purchase train ticket, have it delivered electronically to their mobile phone and stored on the phone's smart card. They will gain access to the platform by waving the phone at the ticket barrier. Furthermore, they will be able to do the same whether they are commuting in the UK or visiting Japan.

### OPINION POLLING

26. Individuals will be able to vote on issues of the day quickly and simply by responding to a question sent to the mobile phone, using the SMS (short message service) facility. It will be possible for pollsters, and the Government if it so wishes, to canvas the views of the population on an unprecedented scale. In the longer term, when electronic signatures are accepted, it will be possible for people to vote in local, national or European elections via their mobile phones and without leaving home—something which could encourage more widespread voting. They will even be able to do it as electronic postal voters if they are overseas on business or holiday.

### PURCHASE OF GOODS AND SERVICES

27. A person visiting a town for the first time could request information on local areas of interest and current events, and in future view a short video clip of the attraction, all via their mobile phone. They could find out opening times, ticket availability and cost, purchase a ticket and receive directions on how to get there.

28. Mobile e-commerce could benefit small local suppliers too. A local supplier may be able to broadcast a message to all phones in the vicinity, for example a special meal promotion, enabling the recipient to order and pay by phone and collect at a drive through.

### MOBILE WALLET

29. It is already possible to perform basic banking transactions such as checking a balance, transfers between accounts and bill payment using special mobile terminals. The next step will enable people to send electronic cash to and from a GSM phone, allowing them to make micropayments using their "electronic purse", or to hold loyalty points and trade them for goods and services. In the longer term, it may be feasible for the Government to pay benefits to people directly into their electronic purse held on their mobile phone.

### SECURE ENVIRONMENT ACCESS

30. Using the security of the mobile phone, people will be able to call or send a short message to activate the door lock of a secured environment, such as a car park or building.

TODAY'S EARLY MOBILE E-COMMERCE

31. For some years people have been carrying out what might be termed early e-commerce transactions using their mobile phones. The purchase of information services via premium rate calls or on subscription, such as sports scores, news, weather or share information, are good examples of early mobile e-commerce. Vodafone's data services subsidiary handles nearly 1 million such transactions per month. It is a small step from providing information in this way to ordering an item via the mobile phone and paying for it on the Vodafone bill. A good example would be the purchase of a phone accessory from Vodafone's retail arm.

32. Vodafone has also recently launched a mobile EPOS terminal. Mobile e-mail will be available within a few months and, with the improvement of text-to-voice technology improvements, e-mails can be read out to people on their mobile phones.

33. In the UK today there are approximately 6 million customers who prepay for their mobile phone service. The balances on their accounts are held as a "cash" balance that is decremented in small amounts as the mobile phone is used. With 2.5 million prepay customers, Vodafone is already a major electronic cash provider, albeit with the balance tied to the use of airtime. This is a forerunner to the networks holding electronic cash for their customers for use in purchasing other small items.

34. In Finland, a mobile operator is trialing a "dial-a-drink" service where the cost of the drink is charged to the customer's telephone bill. The customer dials a telephone number displayed on the front of the vending machine, the call is relayed to a GSM telephone contained in the machine and this activates the dispensing mechanism. Similar services include the dial-a-car-wash and dial-a-jukebox. Although in their infancy, applications of this type are important because they enable e-commerce without the service supplier providing special electronic equipment at his supply point, and without the user having to carry and learn how to use new technology. To the user it is just a call for a cup of coffee.

THE VODAFONE GROUP

1. The Vodafone Group is currently the UK's eighth largest company with a market capitalisation in excess of £35 billion. The Group is dedicated to the provision of mobile communications services in the UK and 13 countries internationally. It has over 10 million proportionate customers world-wide (on an equity adjusted basis) of whom nearly half are overseas. In the UK Vodafone is market leader and currently provides service to 37 per cent of cellular users. It recently led the introduction of prepayment tariffs in the UK creating an explosion in uptake amongst groups of people who were previously excluded from ownership of a mobile phone.

Once Vodafone's merger with AirTouch is completed, the combined Group will be truly global with a strong voice in the UK, Europe, the US and the Far East. It will have operations in 24 countries and over 27 million customers. Vodafone AirTouch will become the second or third largest UK Company with a market capitalisation over £70 billion and will have its headquarters here in the UK. The combined Group will be the world's premier wireless company and one of the world's top 10 telecommunications companies by market capitalisation.

2. The Company continues to invest heavily in the development of its UK network, this year expected to be around £350 million. It plans to introduce new technology for enhancing data speeds over the network in 2000 and to invest in new third generation technology. Vodafone has established a *"centre of expertise"* in e-commerce, involving experts in product development, technology, engineering, retailing and marketing. It has a research programme that places considerable emphasis on new applications of mobile technology, not least on e-commerce, new methods of payment and customer personalisation of services.

3. Vodafone executives participate actively on various Government inquiries including the Information Age Partnership, the Information Society Initiative, the ICT Strategy, the PIU Unit and e-commerce. Vodafone welcomes the opportunity to participate in these debates.

## APPENDIX 5

### Memorandum submitted by OFTEL

INTRODUCTION

1. The purpose of this further memorandum is to update the Committee on developments since OFTEL's original submission and to comment briefly on a number of issues which have been raised with the Committee by other respondents.

OFTEL's Goal of Promoting Consumers' Interests

2. OFTEL considers that it is useful to re-iterate that our goal is to ensure that consumers get the best deal from telecoms companies in terms of quality, choice and value for money. We take this objective very seriously. We agree that an important aspect of consumer choice is the ability to choose from a variety of tariffs—including packages of higher line rentals and cheaper or unmetered call charges advocated by other respondents.

3. OFTEL considers that the best way of delivering our goal is to ensure strong, sustainable competition in both services and infrastructure in the telecommunications industry. Effective competition ensures that companies act to provide the best possible services to their customers.

4. We believe that regulatory intervention should be aimed at promoting competition where it is weak or unlikely to develop without OFTEL action and protecting consumers where competition is not yet effective. Competition is the spur to development of, for example, innovative tariffs to offer consumers greater choice. Regulation should be the minimum necessary, since there are costs to regulation. It can distort market incentives and behaviour in a way which may jeopardise innovation and longer term development of markets and, thereby, consumers' long term interests.

OFTEL's Commitment to Consultation and Transparency

5. OFTEL is also committed to developing policy with a maximum of dialogue with interested parties and transparency in how decisions are reached. OFTEL stands ready to discuss policy issues with interested parties. All major policy initiatives are subject to open and detailed consultation as can be seen by looking at the list of consultation documents on OFTEL's Web site. We are happy to share our knowledge with outside organisations in order to identify and avoid misunderstandings about the telecommunications industry in the UK and OFTEL's role. We have regular meetings with industry bodies such as ISPA (Internet Service Provider Association), and LINX (London Internet Exchange), as well as meetings with individual Internet Service Providers (ISPs). OFTEL has recently set up an Internet Forum open to anyone with an interest in the Internet including suppliers, operators, service providers, government, consumer groups etc. OFTEL has also met with consumer groups such as CUT on a number of occasions, and has a continuing dialogue with such groups in person and via email.

6. One criticism which has been made is that OFTEL is too reliant on information provided by BT in taking decisions and that this information is not available to third parties. For reasons of effective regulation, OFTEL may not be able to release some commercially confidential information about firms' businesses that we receive. However, in BT's case OFTEL has spent many years developing a system of separated regulatory accounts. These provide a great deal of information about BT's costs and revenues, broken down at a higher level of disaggregation, than would be available from statutory accounts. The information in these accounts is required to be independently audited. The Regulatory Accounts are published annually and are available from BT. Where this information is insufficient—for example in a particular competition investigation, OFTEL can and does ask for information in much greater detail. We have considerable experience and expertise in scrutinising such data.

Market Developments in the Price of Dial-Up Internet Access

7. Using the Internet via a dial-up connection (ie via a telephone line and modem, as opposed to a leased line connection) involves the use of two main services. First, there are the services provided by the ISP which include access to the World Wide Web, e-mail, Web-page hosting, etc. Second, there is the use of the Public Switched Telephone Network (PSTN) to dial up an ISP. In the past year, there have been significant developments in charges to consumers for both services.

8. First, since the launch of Dixon's *Freeserve* last year there has been an explosion in the number of subscription-free ISPs. A recent listing of these ISPs on a Web site (www.n4n.co.uk) identified around 150 subscription-free ISPs. The subscription-free ISP has also been credited with stimulating an increase in the percentage of the population in the UK with Internet access. A new survey by Datamonitor and NOP indicates that nearly 20 per cent of the adult population in the UK now have Internet access through a home computer, compared with 15 per cent in Germany, five per cent in France and eight per cent in Italy. The ratio of homes with computers which use them to access the Internet is 2:1 in the UK, 3:1 in Germany and 4:1 in France, Italy and Spain. (Exact comparisons with the US are not available. In the US 35–40 per cent of households have access to the Internet through a home computer).

9. Second, there have also been some significant moves to offer consumers alternative ways of paying for dial-up Internet access other than through metered calls. A number of service providers now allow off-peak dial-up access to the Internet via 0800 free-phone numbers. LocalTel, a Surrey based telco has begun offering unmetered off-peak calls. X-stream, a subscription-free ISP offers unmetered access at certain off-peak times such as late at night and at weekends (the only cost being an advertising banner across the top of the screen). BT Internet and F9 Premier, which are subscription-based services, have also begun offering their customers unmetered access at weekends. There is much speculation about other similar services which may begin in the near future (see www.n4n.co.uk/freecallinfo.htm).

10. OFTEL welcomes these developments. We consider that the rapid changes which are taking place are indicative of a competitive market. In this context, we believe that regulatory intervention to require changes to tariff structures would be inappropriate. The market is already beginning to deliver the choice consumers want. OFTEL takes the view that the appropriate structure of tariffs is a commercial decision best left to companies themselves—provided, of course, that any proposed tariffs meet the terms and conditions of an operator's licence. In BT's case, this means that we need to be assured that any changes are not anti-competitive or discriminate unfairly between customers.

11. Tariffs are most likely to be found to be anti-competitive if they do not cover the costs of the services to which they relate, ie they result in BT incurring losses which it has to cover from other parts of its business. Such cross-subsidies could prevent other operators from competing effectively, thereby diminishing choices for consumers. Tariffs would be likely to be found to discriminate unfairly between customers if they resulted in significant cross-subsidisation between classes of customers—for example if high charges to one group of customers were used to support low charges to another type of customer.

12. OFTEL continues to monitor market developments and discuss with telcos and ISPs potential barriers to further innovation in tariffs. A number of parties have argued that unmetered tariffs are untenable as long as interconnection charges are time based. It should be noted that, although interconnection payments are generally time based (some flat rate charges are available, eg to provide Internet access to schools) OFTEL does not mandate that charges should be time based. We acknowledge that providing unmetered calls for a fixed with metered interconnection presents significant risks for operators because the amount of revenue from fees from consumers might be insufficient to meet interconnection charges if usage is higher than expected. Operators are free to come to commercial agreements which mitigate this risk, provided that charges meet licence conditions. In BT's case, this would mean that charges would need to conform to Network Charge Controls, that they were offered on a non-discriminatory basis and that they were not anti-competitive. The scope for facilitating different bases for interconnection payments is an issue that we intend to examine as part of the review of controls on BT's interconnection charges which is now getting underway.

OFTEL CONSULTATION PAPER ON THE RELATIONSHIP BETWEEN RETAIL PRICES AND INTERCONNECTION CHARGES FOR NUMBER TRANSLATION SERVICES

13. In March OFTEL published a consultation paper titled *The Relationship between Retail Prices and Interconnection Charges for Number Translation Services* (Annex 1). NTS services are those which use "non-geographic" number ranges such as 0800, 0345, 0990 etc. Calls to these numbers, instead of being sent to a specific geographic location, are routed intelligently within the PSTN to an appropriate destination. These number ranges have specific tariffs associated with them, eg 0345/0845 calls are charged at an operator's local rate. When a call to an 0345/0845 NTS number starts on one operator's network (the originating operator) and ends on another (the terminating operator) the revenue received by the originating operator must be shared with the terminating operator (ie there needs to be an interconnection payment). The rule governing the distribution of revenue when BT is the originating operator (the "NTS formula"), which tends to be followed by other operators as well, is set by OFTEL. Currently, BT is allowed only to retain an amount equal to its costs (including a mark-up to recover retail costs) for originating NTS calls.

14. These issues are highly relevant to the issue of dial-up Internet access as most calls of this type now use local-rate NTS (0345/0845 numbers), which means that they are charged at operators' prices for local calls. Furthermore, most dial-up calls to the Internet start on BT's network and end on other operator's networks. The restriction on BT's origination retention has been the key factor behind the development of subscription-free ISPs such as *Freeserve*. This is because the revenue passed through to terminating operators has proven sufficient to cover their costs and also enable a share of the call revenue to be passed to the ISP. This has enabled ISPs to fund their activities out of their share of call revenue (as well as other income sources).

15. OFTEL's review of the NTS interconnection formula was part of a wider review of the issue of whether terminating operators/service providers should have a greater say in the charges consumers pay to dial up their services. OFTEL was concerned that the effect of the NTS formula (together with the restricted number of retail "price points" which BT offered) is to restrict price competition between service providers. In the case of Internet access, for example, it has become something of a truism that dial-up Internet access should be at priced at local call charges. There is no inherent reason why this should be the case.

16. BT has recently increased the number of NTS price points available from 63 to 99. It plans to increase this to 9,999 by the end of the year. OFTEL proposed that, as more price points become available, the NTS formula should be replaced by a system where service providers choose the price of calls to their services. In the case of Internet access, we consider that this will increase the socpe for tariff innovation and, potentially, lower prices to consumers (for exampe if a fall in ISP costs justify lower charges).

17. OFTEL also proposed that BT's retention should remain limited to its network and retail costs until the next price control review. This ensures that Internet access provision can continue to be financed from call revenue in the foreseeable future.

INTERNATIONAL COMPARISONS

18. The international relative position of UK consumers and business in terms of the cost of using the Internet is an important issue in respect of the development of e-commerce and the UK's competitiveness. OFTEL reported to the Committee the results of work produced for the OECD which shows that at peak times the cost of use of subscription free services in the UK is near the average cost of Internet use in OECD countries, while at off-peak times it is significantly below the average.

19. OFTEL is undertaking further internal research on various aspects of the cost of using the Internet and supplying Internet access in the UK compared with other countries. This will enable us to obtain a clearer picture of where the UK stands—in terms of the current situation and developing trends, in an international context. This work is progressing in parallel with OFTEL's ongoing work on monitoring the comparative price of leased lines in the UK as against other countries. OFTEL will publish an analysis of leased line prices later this summer.

20. The benchmark used by many commentators for comparing the cost of Internet access is, clearly, the United States. In doing so, it is useful to bear in mind a number of relevant features of the US environment. First, while there are clearly common features, much telecoms regulation applies at a State level. There are significant variations in regulation and commercial practice across the US. Comparisons between the UK and only one or two US states can therefore present an artificial picture of the relative position of consumers in the UK as against US consumers.

21. Second, while Internet access for US consumers with unmetered local calls is very cheap, their overall cost of telecoms services may not be. It is generally accepted that unmetered calling within local exchange zones has, in the past, been supported by cross subsidies from long distance to local services[8]. Cross subsidies were fostered by regulatory decisions. Since the divestiture of ATT US federal policy has been to remove these cross-subsidies by raising the fixed local charges (via a "Subscriber Line Charge" set initially at $1 per line per month for residential and single-line business subscribers, now $3.50 per line per month) and reducing charges long distance carriers are required to pay LECs.

22. Furthermore, Americans pay on a per minute basis for calls to all areas outside local exchange zones. In general, these zones tend to cover relatively small areas, A recent study by Eurodata[9] found both that there is considerable variation in the cost consumers face for using a specific basket of telecoms services across the US and that this basket can cost more in some US states than in some European countries. The costs for BT customers of the basket of services (which was the highest cost of the four European countries included in the survey) were lower than the costs to consumers in 8 out of the 10 US states included in the study.[10]

23. It is important to emphasise that OFTEL does not consider that these factors demonstrate that unmetered calling or cross-subsidies between different types of calls are inherently undesirable. As noted above, we welcome new tariffs which meet the needs of consumers and which are commercially justified, We point out these issues in order to ensure that comparisons are made with the US system in a balanced manner.


RATIONALE FOR TIME-BASED CHARGES

24. A number of respondents to the Committee argue that time-based charging for telephone calls, in general, is inappropriate. The predominant method of dial-up access to the Internet in the UK at present, is via the PSTN. A call to the Internet uses the PSTN in just the same way as a normal telephone call.

25. The view that charging by time for use of the PSTN is inappropriate relies on the view that costs are not caused by the duration of calls. However, three fundamental features of the PSTN mean that, at peak times, duration should be taken into account when pricing calls. First, in a circuit switched network such as the PSTN each pair of users requires a circuit which remains dedicated to their communication for the duration of the call. Second, capacity needs to be sufficient to cope with demand at peak times on the basis of an acceptable quality of service. Finally, in a switched network, additional circuits are relatively expensive to provide.

26. These features mean that, at peak times, callers generate a cost by tying up capacity. When all circuits are being used, other callers cannot make calls. The extent of this cost is, therefore, related to the duration of the calls. Charging callers on a basis which reflects this cost encourages efficient use of the network. It also ensures that the owner faces the right incentives to invest in the network. Capacity will be expanded when the cost of adding circuits is less than the revenue expected to be earned from those circuits.

27. This argument does not apply in quite the same way at off-peak times, when demand is well below capacity. However, charging very low prices, or providing unmetered calls, in off-peak periods will increase usage at those times. Potentially, demand could increase at the (formerly) off-peak times to such an extent that usage becomes similar to levels at peak times thereby giving rise to the congestion problems which

---

[8] See, for example, *Competition and Tariffs in the USA, A Report by Eurodata Foundation*, February 1999, p14, or *Toward Competition in Local Telephony*, W J Baumol and J G Sidak (1994), MIT Press, p125.

[9] *ibid.*

[10] The states which had higher costs were New York, Kansas, Georgia, Florida, Ohio, Pennsylvania, Minnesota and Texas. The other states were California and Illinois. The four European countries included in the survey were UK, France, Sweden, Denmark, Norway.

underlie time-based charging. Whether it would be the case that demand would increase to this extent with very low prices or unmetered charging is an empirical/network planning issue.

28. The Internet itself does not suffer to the same extent the "peak load" issue which arises in respect of the PSTN. The Internet uses packet switched networks which do not use dedicated circuits for conveying messages. Data transmitted over IP networks are sent in small "packets" which can be transmitted separately, to be re-assembled into the original message at the destination. This enables more efficient use of available bandwidth than the PSTN.

## FUTURE DEVELOPMENTS

29. A number of new developments are currently underway which are aimed at reducing the extent to which the PSTN is the main method of reaching the Internet. This will enable the problems associated with this method of Internet access, outlined above, to be reduced and, ultimately, avoided.

30. First, telecoms companies will make Internet calls traverse their networks more efficiently. For historical reasons, calls to the Internet are generally national calls charged at a local rate. This is obviously an inefficient use of resources, as a large number of network elements are tied up across the PSTN for the complete duration of the call. Telecoms companies, including BT, are planning on moving their Internet access points closer to the edge of their networks, so as to reduce the number of network elements used.

31. More importantly, there will soon be wider avaliability of access to the Internet via higher bandwidth services, such as cable modems and xDSL technologies. These technologies will enable "always on" connection to the Internet and, because of their relative lack of the capacity problems associated with the PSTN, are usually offered without time-based tariffs. Access via cable networks has been started by one company (NTL) and is expected soon on the networks of the other two cable companies (CWC and Telewest). There is currently a great deal of speculation that BT will begin offering ADSL services in the near future. As discussed in our previous submission, OFTEL is currently consulting on whether BT should be required to provide access to its local loop to encourage competitive provision of xDSL services. We expect to announce the results of this consultation very shortly.

32. Other higher bandwidth technologies which currently exist, or will be used in the future include satellite and terrestrial wireless access and third generation mobile access. Satellite and terrestrial wireless access are both currently offered in the UK. For example, Datalink (www.data-link.co.uk) offers satellite Internet access while Tele2 UK (www.alwayson.co.uk) offers terrestrial wireless access via its Advanced Digital Wireless network. Third-generation mobile services that will allow Internet access are due to be launched in the UK by January 1, 2002.

## PSTN CONGESTION

33. OFTEL has been asked to expand on the point in paragraph 33 of our previous submission concerning the potential for unmetered calling to have an impact on network congestion. As discussed above, as a circuit switched network, the PSTN is designed to handle a limited number of callers at any one time. The design of the network's capacity is based on assumptions about the number and duration of calls which will be made. If large numbers of consumers tie up circuits for long periods of time, this increases the risk that circuits will not be available to other users. At the limit, other users may be prevented from making calls.

34. OFTEL is aware that the issue of the impact of unmetered dial-up access to the Internet on local-loop congestion has been a topic of hot debate in the United States. It is important to distinguish in this debate between congestion in call origination and termination. The commonly cited example of AOL not being able to cope with calls to its services when it moved to flat-rate charging in 1997 is an example of congestion in call termination. This results because the firm in question does not purchase sufficient lines or install sufficient modems for consumers to reach them. It is less of a public policy issue than congestion in call origination because the company bears the consequences of its under-investment—through consumer dissatisfaction and cancelled subscriptions.

35. The debate in the the US about the effect of Internet use on congestion in the local loop has been between incumbent local exchange carriers (ILECs) such as Pacific Bell and Bell Atlantic, representatives of consumer interests and ISPs. This is because ILECs have advocated raising charges for calls to the Internet as a means of dealing with congestion problems in call origination. OFTEL does not have access to the studies of congestion allegedly caused by Internet use prepared for ILECs. Some studies are referred to in a submission by the Commercial Internet Exchange (CIX) to the FCC in March 1997 (www.cix.org/noi0397.html).

36. It is also possible to find anecdotal evidence of call failure in sources on the Internet. For example a Seattle Times article from January 1998 reports complaints to the Washington state regulator about the inability to complete telephone calls which is ascribed to Internet use (www.seattletimes.com/news/business/html98/fone_012398.html, also at Annex 2). This year the regulator in New Hampshire set up an investigation into "congestion on the public switched telephone network (PSTN) caused by the proliferation of Internet usage" (www.puc.state.nh.us/99020ont.html, also at Annex 3). This follows increased levels of consumer complaints about the inability to complete calls.

37. Evidence given by opponents of the ILECs' position does not deny such problems, but denies that they are widespread (being limited to the United States' most heavily computer-oriented communities, such as Silicon Valley and Reston/Herndon). Studies of the effect of heavy Internet use on PSTN networks in these areas have been undertaken by Pacific Telesis and Bell Atlantic respectively and submitted to the FCC. Opponents of the ILECs' position also deny that congestion problems require regulatory intervention. For example at a FCC forum in 1997 the Vice President of Operations and Vice President of America Online Networks, Matthew R Korn, stated that:

> "Even in the few instances where there have been problems, there appear to be technological and engineering answers." (www.fcc.gov/bandwidth/korn.txt)

Similarly, in the CIX filing referred to above, it is stated that:

> "with the abundance of local digital access networks entering the market in the near term, the problem of "network congestion" is temporal at best"[11] (www.cix.org/noi0397.html).

SUMMARY

— OFTEL is committed to ensuring that consumers receive the best deal in terms of quality, choice and value for money.

— We believe that the best way of achieving this is through sustainable competition

— We consider that there is strong competition in the provision of dial-up access to the Internet and that regulatory intervention in this area could be counterproductive.

— OFTEL welcomes the recent innovation in tariff packages which offer consumers more choice.

— We consider that competition will continue to deliver benefits to consumers, both in terms of the pricing of Internet access and the introduction of new high bandwidth technologies which avoid the problems associated with the use of the PSTN for access.

— We are committed to removing impediments to sustainable competition in the market. Our consultation documents on interconnection charges for NTS services and access to bandwidth address regulatory and market impediments to competition.

— Comparisons with other countries, in particular the US, need to be taken with care as they don't necessarily give the full picture.

— Nevertheless, it is important to benchmark progress in the UK and we are continuing to work on comparisons between the UK and other countries in a number of areas related to the Internet.

*30 June 1999*

## APPENDIX 6

### Extract from memorandum submitted by the Post Office[12]

**Annex 3**

Research indicates that citizens are increasingly willing to try electronic channels to interact more effectively with Government. However, they insist that these new channels should supplement and not replace traditional channels and the acceptance of technology is significantly lower for the older and poorer sections of society.

The Post Office, which enjoys exceptionally high ratings for accessibility, familiarity, service, and trust, and is seen as a natural provider of Government services, is ideally suited to form the backbone of the "Better Government" agenda and act as a single provider of all types of channels, using sub-contractors as necessary for particular expertise. The Post Office's capability to deliver to every door and provide 19,000 Post Offices Counter outlets within one mile of 94 per cent of the population are valued by all, particularly the old, the poor and those living in rural communities. In addition The Post Office has one of the largest customer bases in the UK, involving communication with most UK businesses every day. These capabilities are continually being built upon by harnessing technology in ways that will improve services and accessibility still further and provide a key enabling infrastructure towards the Information Age within the UK.

Post Office Counters Limited are in the process of automating all Post Offices as part of the Horizon project, which will see the installation of approximately 40,000 touch screen terminals that will be networked and linked to central systems via an open, Internet-enabled and secure architecture. The initial applications are the payment of benefits and the automation of existing Government processes such as National Savings, Passport Agency, DVLA, and others, although the scope and extent of this project will increase in time.

---

[11] OFTEL notes that CIX do not consider that there is a network congestion problem.
[12] See Trade and Industry Committees 7th Report, Session 1998–99, HC187, "Building Confidence in Electronic Commerce": The Governments proposals p151.

The exchange of services and information between citizens and Government in most key policy areas could be improved dramatically through Horizon. The combination of the Post Office's existing brand values, reach and ability to combine traditional and electronic channels can ensure that "Information Age Government" is achieved more quickly and in a socially inclusive way. Examples of these possible services include the following:

— Open Government: Postal and electronic polling; improving central and local Government consultation.

— Health Services: Advice; appointments; donor recruitment and registrations; health record storage and access.

— Welfare Services: Universal Banking; welfare rights advice; fraud prevention.

— Employment: Job opportunities and applications; benefit/grant information.

Education: Information on schools, colleges and other educational institutions on performance and courses; grants information and application.

— Transport: Integrated public transport information and ticketing; payment of road tolls.

— Law and Order: Information on crime prevention; non-violent crime reporting; validation of documents; payment of fines.

This potential future role for the Post Office is currently being demonstrated by the "Open for Business" pilot project. The pilot, which is led and managed by the Post Office, allows small businesses in the Norwich area to obtain relevant and integrated information across a wide range of central and local Government departments and to register their businesses electronically via a digital signature. These diverse services are provided under one common familar and customer focused brand—"Post Office Open For Business". Other, more advanced, applications of this service in the Electronic Commerce market will in due course be investigated and proved.

Printed in the United Kingdom by The Stationery Office Limited
8/99   440646   19585   CRC Supplied.

ISBN 0-10-556306-4

9 780105 563068